Time Out

Edinburgh & Glasgow

Eating & Drinking

timeout.com

Penguin Books

PENGUIN BOOKS

Published by the Penguin Group
Penguin Books Ltd, 80 Strand, London WC2R ORL, England
Penguin Group (USA), Inc., 375 Hudson Street, New York, New York 10014, USA
Penguin Books Australia Ltd, 250 Camberwell Road, Camberwell, Victoria 3124,
    Australia
Penguin Books Canada Ltd, 10 Alcorn Avenue, Toronto, Ontario, Canada M4V 3B2
Penguin Books (NZ) Ltd, cnr Rosedale and Airborne Roads, Albany, Auckland,
    New Zealand

Penguin Books Ltd, Registered Offices: Harmondsworth, Middlesex, England

First published 2003
10 9 8 7 6 5 4 3 2 1

Colour reprographics by Icon, Crowne House, 56-58 Southwark Street, London
SE1 1UN

Printed and bound by Cayfosa-Quebecor, Ctra. de Caldes, Km 3 08 130 Sta,
Perpètua de Mogoda, Barcelona, Spain

Edited and designed by
Time Out Guides Limited
Universal House
251 Tottenham Court Road
London W1T 7AB
Tel + 44 (0)20 7813 3000
Fax + 44 (0)20 7813 6001
Email guides@timeout.com
www.timeout.com

Editorial
Editor Keith Davidson
Deputy Editor Cath Phillips
Glasgow Editors Andrea Mullaney,
  Fiona Shepherd
Listings Editors Shane Armstrong,
  Holly Furneaux
Proofreader Phil Harriss

Editorial Director Peter Fiennes
Series Editor Sarah Guy
Guides Co-ordinator Anna Norman

Design
Group Art Director John Oakey
Art Director Mandy Martin
Art Editor Scott Moore
Senior Designer Tracey Ridgewell
Junior Designers Astrid Kogler, Sam Lands
Picture Editor Kerri Miles
Acting Picture Editor Kit Burnet
Acting Picture Deputy Editor Martha Houghton
Picture Trainee Bella Wood

Digital Imager Dan Conway
Ad Make-up Charlotte Blythe

Advertising
Group Commercial Director Lesley Gill
Sales Director Mark Phillips
International Sales Manager Ross Canadé
Advertisement Sales (Edinburgh & Glasgow)
  Christie Dessy
Advertising Assistant Sabrina Ancilleri

Administration
Chairman Tony Elliott
Managing Director Mike Hardwick
Group Financial Director Richard Waterlow
Group Marketing Director Christine Cort
Marketing Manager Mandy Martinez
US Publicity & Marketing Associate
  Rosella Albanese
Group General Manager Nichola Coulthard
Guides Production Director Mark Lamond
Production Controller Samantha Furniss
Accountant Sarah Bostock

Contributors
Introductions *Eating in Edinburgh & Glasgow* Keith Davidson, Andrea Mullaney. *What is Scottish food?* Burns Night Keith Davidson. *Whisky* Keith Davidson. **Edinburgh reviews & features** Keith Davidson. **Glasgow reviews** Andrea Mullaney, Fiona Shepherd. **Glasgow features** *Coffee, tea and scones; Boozing by Underground; The Curry Mile* Fiona Shepherd. *Made from girders* Andrea Mullaney.

Maps by JS Graphics (john@jsgraphics.co.uk). Edinburgh maps are based on material supplied by Alan Collinson through Copyright Exchange. Glasgow maps on pages 177, 201 & 220 are based on material supplied by The XYZ Digital Map Company.

Photography Héloïse Bergman, except page 59 provided by Harvey Nichols.

Contents

About the guide

The reviews in this guide are based solely on the experiences of Time Out restaurant reviewers. All the restaurants, café-bars, bars and pubs listed were visited anonymously over a period of a few months, and Time Out footed the bills. No payment of any kind from restaurant owners has secured or influenced a review in this guide.

In the listings, the times given are those observed by the kitchen; in other words, the times within which one is fairly certain to be able to sit down and order a meal. These can change according to time of year and the owners' whims, so it is often a good idea to call ahead. It's wise to book for popular and more fashionable restaurants, especially on Fridays and Saturdays. Average prices listed are per person for three courses, excluding drinks and service, and have been graded on the following scale:

up to £15	£
£16 to £25	££
£26 to £35	£££
over £35	££££

We list the credit cards accepted by initials: AmEx (American Express), DC (Diners Club), MC (MasterCard) and V (Visa).

Throughout the guide we've listed phone numbers as dialled from within the city in question. If you're phoning from outside the city, you need to add the area code (0131 for Edinburgh, 0141 for Glasgow).

The star system is to help you identify top performers at a glance. A red star – ★ – by the name of a restaurant means that our reviewers found it to be one of the best in the city.

Eating

in Edinburgh & Glasgow

Edinburgh and Glasgow are Janus-faced when it comes to food and drink. Sometimes the locals have to remind themselves that in comparison to similar-sized English cities such as Leeds, Liverpool or Manchester, the Scottish pair do extremely well in terms of restaurants, café-bars and noteworthy pubs. Then again, jaded foodies in central Scotland gaze mournfully at major European centres and bemoan their lack of choice in terms of truly international-class dining. Strangely enough, both points of view ring true.

In general UK terms, Edinburgh and Glasgow excel. But it's important to remember that Scotland on its own is a small and peripheral nation. Glasgow may well be one of the biggest cities in the British Isles, and Edinburgh ranks among the top six European financial centres (as well as being a capital in its own right), but between them their population barely tops a million. There's no way that these numbers can support the kind of restaurant

culture – or competition between establishments – taken for granted in much more populous locations like London and Paris. Despite this, Edinburgh and Glasgow offer everything from a sprinkling of Michelin-starred eateries to ornate Victorian drinking dens, cutting-edge café-bars, artisan beers and whiskies, and ethnic cuisines as diverse as Thai and Turkish. That's more than enough to keep the average visitor content, while ennui-ridden locals can always pop along to Glasgow's **Amaryllis** (*see p184*) or Edinburgh's **Restaurant Martin Wishart** (*see p85*) for a fix of top-end culinary grooviness once in a while.

Edinburgh

At the west end of Princes Street, Lothian Road strikes off to the south. On the corner sits the Caledonian Hilton Hotel. Once upon a time it was a grand Edwardian railway hotel serving as the terminal pleasure palace for travellers who had journeyed north. But the railway didn't last. The adjacent station was demolished and, as recently as 20 years ago, much of the land around that part of Lothian Road was gap site. (The 'Caley' itself thrived, of course, with its celebrated **Pompadour** restaurant – *see p122*.)

That gap site pretty much reflected the economic condition of the city at the time. Margaret Thatcher was prime minister, unemployment had rocketed in the early 1980s, and it was particularly tough for young people to find work. Two decades later and young people in Edinburgh find it difficult to avoid work – such has been the transformation in economic fortunes.

Nowadays, the west side of Lothian Road has the upmarket Sheraton Hotel (1985), a huge financial services group (Standard Life, 1997-2001) and the swankiest health club in Edinburgh (One, behind the Sheraton, 2001); there's also the Edinburgh International Conference Centre designed by Terry Farrell (1995) and the eye-catching Scottish Widows building along Morrison Street (1998).

The expansion of financial services and related businesses in Edinburgh through the 1990s – not to mention the arrival of Scotland's own parliament – has certainly changed what's possible in terms of food and drink. There's more income and it's being disposed of, especially by twenty- and thirtysomethings.

In the pre-boom years, traditionally moneyed areas like the New Town were able to support a patrician little bar like **Kay's** (*see p72*), while Duddingston had the **Sheep Heid** (*see p115*) and the city centre boasted authentic, long-standing establishments such as the **Guildford Arms** (*see p72*), the **Café Royal** (*see p70*) and **Bennet's** (*see p114*). Such exceptions aside, the drinking scene was otherwise pretty drab. On the food front, restaurateurs like Martin Irons (**Martins**; *see p61*) were

making headway with serious eating from 1983, while the likes of **Skippers** (*see p79*), the **Kalpna** (*see p104*) and **Loon Fung** (*see p52*) were also around in the '80s, so it would be unfair to say that Edinburgh was bereft of decent restaurants. But most of the places listed in this guide certainly didn't exist. What changed?

If there was one establishment that really upped the ante it was the **Atrium** (*see p125*), courtesy of Andrew Radford. It opened in 1993 with design values allied to kitchen standards in a combination that was unprecedented. People who worked there went on to be involved in other excellent city restaurants such as **(fitz)Henry** (*see p83*) and the **Marque** (*see p108*) while Radford even added a café-bar one floor above his flagship eaterie in 1997: **blue bar-café** (*see p127*).

Otherwise, trends in bars have come and gone – just look at the **Basement** (*see p88*) then **Beluga** (*see p35*), then compare and contrast. Meanwhile, the very latest in restaurants seems to involve high design values, grill

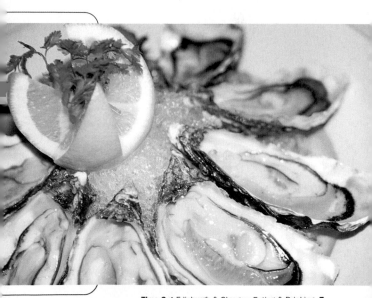

What is Scottish food?

There's one very important thing to remember about Scotland: it's a long way north. Edinburgh and Glasgow, relatively southern cities in Scottish terms, lie at around the same latitude as Moscow, Copenhagen and Labrador in Canada. The Gulf Stream wards off the worst of the chill, but the basic geography means no vineyards, no citrus fruit, no olive groves – you'll certainly be struggling for the basic ingredients of ratatouille. The climate determines the agricultural output, which, in turn, has set much of the historical framework for Scottish cooking.

Going way back, hunting was common (red deer, hare, wildfowl), as was fishing in rivers (trout, salmon) and foraging on the coast for shellfish (mussels). Although barley and beef cattle have long been mainstays of Scottish farming, it was probably the influence of Viking settlers from the eighth to 13th centuries that introduced sea fishing (cod, haddock, herring, mackerel).

A later foreign influence came from further south. Before the Scottish and English crowns merged in 1603, independent Scotland's diplomatic ties with France (the Auld Alliance) had a marked influence on Scottish cooking, particularly for the nobility (rich sauces, cakes, pastries, preserved fruit and desserts) – though little impact on the average peasant living off barley meal, of course.

Meanwhile, items as intimately associated with Scotland as potatoes, swedes (often called neeps or, very confusingly, turnips) and oats didn't really become widespread until the 18th and 19th centuries, their introduction going hand in hand with improvements to agricultural practices. These weren't the only important introductions at that time. After the failure of the Jacobite rebellion in 1745-46 (an attempt to put a Catholic Stuart monarch back on the British throne, replacing the Protestant House of Hanover) came the infamous Highland Clearances where the people were forced off the land to the big cities, or abroad; their replacements were sheep. The result: mutton has been a key part of the Scottish larder for more than 200 years.

Then there's a little market gardening to consider, dairy farming (Scotland makes some fine cheeses) and the Industrial Revolution and the advent of mass food production for the cities. Finally, in the last decades of the 20th century, 'foreign' restaurants opened in Edinburgh and Glasgow (Chinese, Indian, Italian and more), just as supermarkets have come to sell everything from Japanese bento boxes to Kenyan green beans. So here in the 21st century, it's far

from straightforward to ask, 'What is Scottish food?'

There are still many Scots who remember traditional home-cooked dishes that have endured for generations: **porridge** (oats boiled in water to produce a thick nutritious slurry), **Scotch broth** (soup based on mutton stock with root vegetables, barley and pulses), **mince and tatties** (minced beef and mashed potatoes), **stovies** (potatoes stewed in a pan with leftover meat) or **skirlie** (oatmeal fried with onion in lard).

Puddings and cakes include **clootie dumpling** (wheat flour, suet, eggs, dried fruit, sugar, spices and other ingredients, wrapped in a cloth and boiled in water), **Dundee cake** (rich fruitcake) and **shortbread** (a biscuit made from wheat flour, sugar and butter).

These are very much the 'people's foods', of course; if there is a folk memory of a distinctively Scottish cuisine, they form the backbone.

They're the dishes being lost to a generation brought up on supermarket ready-meals and takeaway chicken korma, and their general lack of elegance means they don't sit well on a restaurant menu. ('Your clapshot, madam.' Clapshot is a delicate combination of neeps and tatties mashed together with a soupçon of onion fried in lard. Bon appetit.)

When Scottish restaurants have raided the historical cookbook, it has been more for dishes that don't look out of place on designer crockery: **Cullen skink** is one (creamy smoked haddock soup), **cranachan** another (a dessert made with cream, oatmeal, whisky and raspberries). Meanwhile, cutting out 'the people's cuisine' and heading straight for the raw materials means chefs in 'Scottish' restaurants are free to do pretty much what they want. No one's Scottish granny ever cooked them oak-smoked salmon and leek tart with white wine and mussel sauce ('Ye'll hae stovies and like it!'), but you'll find it on the menu at some establishments.

So Scottish food? At home, it's curry and pizza just like everywhere else in the UK; in some restaurants, it's the odd traditional dish, but mainly lots of local ingredients given a contemporary spin. Good ingredients, mind you – and you can't beat a bowl of decent Cullen skink.

menus and attached cocktail bars (**Rogue**, *see p126*;
Oloroso, *see p62*; and **Hurricane Bar & Grill**, *see p59*).
All of which has expanded Edinburgh's dining and drinking
options beyond recognition.

Glasgow

Glasgow, it can safely be said, does not have a reputation
as one of the world's healthiest cities – in fact, its
inhabitants can boast (or not) the highest rate of coronary
heart disease in western Europe, a fact usually blamed
on their traditional diet of fatty, greasy foods. And so it's
perhaps hard to blame any prospective visitor for feeling
that all Scotland's largest city has to offer in the way of
food and drink will be stodgy pies, deep-fried Mars bars
and cans of Tennent's Special.

But while it may not have the profile of other 'foodie'
cities, Glasgow's restaurant and bar scene is actually
one of the liveliest in Britain, with as much choice and
variety as you'll find anywhere outside London. It's
been particularly vibrant in the past decade or so, as

the city, which entered a new phase of confidence and increasing wealth symbolised by its reign as European City of Culture in 1990, threw off many of the old habits of the past and reinvented itself.

The arrival of celebrity chefs such as Gordon Ramsay (**Amaryllis**; *see p184*) and Nick Nairn (**Nairns**; *see p189*) has only sped up the process of improved quality, style and class in Glasgow's restaurants, as exciting new venues open up all the time – the latest pair to be announced, at the time of writing, was a Conran double whammy of a new French restaurant and a Zinc Bar & Grill. Meanwhile, venerable old stagers like the **Buttery** (*see p188*) and the **Ubiquitous Chip** (*see p192*) seem to have taken on a renewed lease of life. And style bars are a phenomenon that many Glaswegians, with their love for dressing up in designer togs, have embraced.

There are still plenty of unpretentious venues, though: old men's pubs with their distinctive atmosphere; historic bars where folk musicians strum their stuff; friendly local cafés and restaurants; and one-off hip hangouts.

As for cuisine, there are venues to suit practically all tastes, whether you're craving something familiar or a new exotic mix. Immigrants from Italy and the Indian

Burns Night

Sales of haggis go through the roof for Burns Night (25 January), when Scotland celebrates its national bard. Peoples all over the world have been eating bits of animal boiled in its own skin since ancient times, but Robert 'Rabbie' Burns' poem, 'Address to a Haggis', helped fix the Scottish version in cultural aspic. The traditional Burns Night meal involves haggis, mashed potatoes and mashed neeps – plus lashings of whisky, of course.

Haggis – 'Great chieftain o the puddin'-race!' in Burns' immortal words – is a mix of assorted sheep viscera, oatmeal, suet, onion and pepper, all wrapped in a sheep's stomach and boiled. It's astonishingly good (and there are fine veggie versions too), but most Scots don't bother to eat it for the other 364 days of the year. Some restaurants in Edinburgh and Glasgow put on a full-blown Burns Supper, but Burns Night is mainly a domestic celebration.

subcontinent, who came over in the last century, built up strongholds in the food business, and fish and chips, pizza and curry are now as much a part of Glaswegian cookery as haggis and neeps – and certainly eaten a darn sight more often. Asian and Mexican food are also popular, while a recent trend has seen local chefs make a point of using fine quality Scottish produce, but prepared and

cooked with modern European techniques and dressings, to create a sophisticated yet still traditional taste.

One great advantage of going out in Glasgow is its size: it's compact enough to make it easy to stagger home afterwards no matter how much you've scoffed or drunk, but large enough to ensure you could visit a different establishment every night for months.

Whisky

As far as the rest of the world is concerned, Scotland *is* whisky; few other countries are so readily identified by a national spirit. Given that just under £2.3bn worth of whisky was shipped to around 200 countries in 2001, it's not hard to see why. The USA, Spain, France, South Korea and Japan are the main buyers, with blended whiskies, rather than single malts, leading the export drive. That still leaves around ten per cent of total production for UK consumption. Not bad for something that started centuries ago in the Scottish countryside...

Beginnings

The first recorded reference to distilling in Scotland dates back to the late 15th century. Some say Irish monks brought the technique with them when they sailed across the water to evangelise pagan Caledonia; others insist that the natives just worked it out for themselves. Either way, for hundreds of years anyone with the know-how and the materials could knock up some usquebaugh (Gaelic for 'the water of life') in an outhouse or wherever else there was space – with complete freedom. Whisky-making was unregulated and quality and taste varied from

area to area. Big country houses would have their own small still, while crofters and farmers might make an occasional batch.

So when the authorities hit on the bright idea of taxing whisky in the mid 17th century, Scots were not best pleased. But it was after the Act of Union in 1707, when

Scotland merged with its southern neighbour, that all hell broke loose. A rationalisation of spirit duties across the new Great Britain saw Scots take to illegal distilling as a patriotic duty, giving it the firmest of footings in the national consciousness. ('Ye can tak oor freedom, but ye cannae tak oor whisky!') Legally speaking, chaos reigned for over 100 years.

The Excise Act of 1823, passed by parliament in London, finally sorted out the tax issues and allowed legal distilling for commercial operations in return for an annual fee, and a sensible level of duty. The result was that small-scale distilling petered out and the production of Scotch finally became a respectable business.

England and the growing British Empire provided the custom for the fledgling industry. But those in charge decided that the patchy, robust and characterful qualities of old usquebaugh were uncommercial and too assertive for such sensitive palates. Instead, whiskies from various distilleries would be blended together to create a lighter, more consistent and balanced drink.

The bulk of the blend – as much as two-thirds – would be grain whisky: less substantial, cheaper to produce and made from unmalted barley or other grains in a process that was far more industrial than the 'rustic' production of usquebaugh. The other third was a careful mix of spirits, what now would be described as single malts, from distilleries around Scotland.

All the way through the 19th century, and for most of the 20th, single malts were simply the building blocks for popular blends. Their production, however, was essentially the same as old usquebaugh.

How do they do that?

First, take barley and soak it in water. Then drain off the water, lay the barley on the floor of a shed and let it germinate. During this process, which can take up to a week, starches turn into sugars. The sprouted barley is then scooped up and dried off. Traditionally this is done over peat fires, which is where some whiskies get their smoky and peaty flavours. The dried grain is then ground up and mixed with hot water to leech out the sugars. The resulting liquid is piped into vats, yeast added, and left to ferment in much the same way as beer.

After fermentation, you have a liquid with low alcohol content all ready for distillation: boiling inside a copper still. Alcohol evaporates at a lower temperature to water, so it's possible to collect the resulting alcohol-rich spirit (well over 60 per cent by volume) and run it off. At this stage, it has no colour and can't even legally be described as whisky (it has to mature for three years first).

But this is the basis of all single malts: whiskies made exclusively from malted barley, the output of one named distillery. Lots of casks eventually get vatted together to make a production run (diluted with water to 40 per cent alcohol by volume for most brands), so even a single malt involves some mixing. But anything marketed as a ten-year-old Glenkinchie, for example, won't contain any other whiskies, and it won't have anything in it that has matured for less than ten years.

One of the wonders of Scotch is how one small country can produce a spirit that has such incredible variety. The local water supply, the shape of the still, the kind of cask the whisky is stored in (giving colour and flavours), where it's stored and the maturation period all make an enormous difference to the final result. For example, Dalmore made at Alness on the Cromarty Firth, which is aged for 12 years in barrels formerly used for bourbon, looks, smells and tastes very different from the Macallan, which is created at Aberlour, inland Banffshire, and aged for ten years in former sherry casks.

Where to buy whisky

Depending on where you go, and what you want, a 70cl bottle of Scotch could cost anything from around a tenner to £75 and above. At the under-£15 end of the market, you're looking at blended whiskies. Scotland's favourite blend is the **Famous Grouse**, although many people find it a little sweet. More interesting choices would be smooth **J&B Rare** or **Black Bottle**, which features single malts from Islay, so has obvious peat and maritime character.

In the £15-£20 bracket come some of the more affordable single malts and deluxe blends, such as **Johnny Walker Black Label** and **Chivas Regal**. Go into any bar from Los Angeles to Lagos and ask for 'a good whisky' and you'll probably be given one of these. Johnny Walker Black is a little on the medicinal side, Chivas Regal less so; they're both a cut above the cheaper blends.

Up to £25 or so, you should be able to get some classic and popular single malts such as 12-year-old **Glenfiddich** from Speyside (nicely sweet and malty), 12-year-old **Highland Park** from Orkney (smoke and toffee) or a trenchant ten-year-old **Ardbeg** from Islay (peat and antiseptic).

Over £25 and you're generally looking at special bottlings or single malt superstars, such as 16-year-old **Lagavulin** from Islay (the experience of a sweet Hebridean bog in your head, at 43 per cent abv).

Past the £30 mark, you'll encounter cask bottlings. This is where a special shop or whisky club buys a specific cask from a distillery and bottles the contents in a limited-edition run. In such rarefied territory, prices soon start to inflate. In early 2003 the **Scotch Malt Whisky Society** of Edinburgh (*see p97*) laid its hands on a 30-year-old cask of single malt from a distillery on Deeside. Only 166 bottles were produced, which were sold to the society's members only for £75 each.

The society is a great place to buy rare malts (bottles start at around £35), and the cost of membership isn't too prohibitive. Members can also try cask whiskies by the glass at the society's premises in Leith. Listed below are other specialist whisky shops. The **Oddbins** outlet on Edinburgh's Royal Mile (223 High Street, 220 3516/www.oddbins.com) also has a great selection of single malts to cater to the passing tourist trade.

If you want to visit a distillery, **Glenkinchie** (01875 342004/www.malts.com) near the village of Pencaitland, East Lothian, is about 15 miles from Edinburgh. The closest to Glasgow, around 12 miles, is **Glengoyne** (01360 550254/www.glengoyne.com) at Dumgoyne, Stirlingshire. Both have visitor centres and run tours and tastings.

Cadenhead's

172 Canongate, Royal Mile, Old Town, Edinburgh (556 5864/www.wmcadenhead. com). **Open** 10.30am-5.30pm Mon-Sat (extended hrs & Sun in Aug). **Credit** MC, V.
A well-established shop on the Royal Mile where the staff know their stuff backwards. Lots of rare whiskies and cask bottlings that you'll find nowhere else.

Royal Mile Whiskies

379 High Street, Royal Mile, Old Town, Edinburgh (225 3383/www.royalmilewhiskies. com). **Open** *Sept-July* 10am-6pm Mon-Sat; 12.30-6pm Sun. *Aug* 10am-8pm Mon-Sat; 12.30-8pm Sun. **Credit** AmEx, MC, V.
Perhaps the most obvious whisky shop on the Royal Mile and certainly the most tourist-oriented. Located opposite St Giles Cathedral, it sells all the popular single malts, special bottlings and cask-strength examples. A tad expensive.

The Whisky Shop

Princes Square, 48 Buchanan Street, City centre, Glasgow (226 8446/www.thewhisky shop.com). **Open** 9.30am-6pm Mon-Wed, Fri, Sat; 9.30am-8pm Thur; 12.30-5pm Sun. **Credit** AmEx, MC, V.
Housed in Glasgow's most upmarket shopping mall, with a large range of the most popular Scottish malts (plus Irish and American brands). The Buchanan Galleries shop is slightly larger and perhaps a little more informal.
Branch: Buchanan Galleries, 220 Buchanan Street, City centre (331 0022).

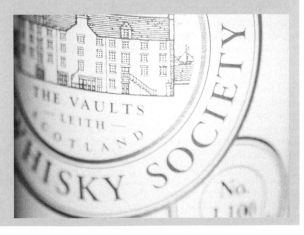

Extra cachet

From the creation of the modern industry right up to the 1960s, the notion of selling the output of an individual distillery as a premium product either didn't occur or was seen as a little loopy. Upmarket whiskies had traditionally been the deluxe blends where the constituent single malts were always at least 12 years old (Johnny Walker Black Label is a current example), while the cheaper blends would use younger single malts (big sellers today are the Famous Grouse, Bell's and J&B Rare).

But in 1963 the independent Glenfiddich distillery, at Dufftown in Banffshire, made a bid for recognition and started to sell its single malt in trademark triangular green bottles. Much to the industry's surprise, Glenfiddich was seen to have even more individuality and cachet than its deluxe blended cousins, so the big firms that own the bulk of Scottish distilleries jumped on the bandwagon, notably from the 1980s.

There are now upwards of 80 single malts on the market, not counting special bottlings. They account for up to 15 per cent of all whisky sales, but old habits die hard: the vast majority of Scotch sold is still the blended variety.

Edinburgh: Old Town

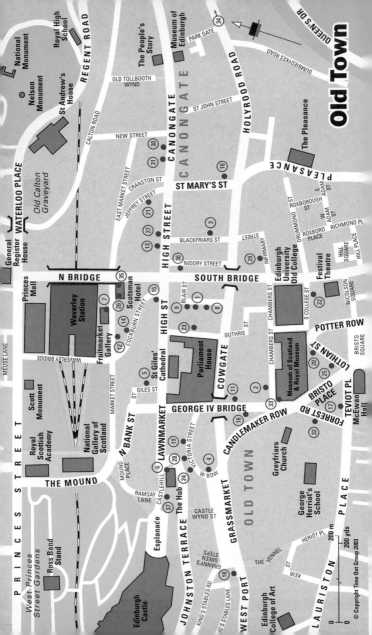

MAP KEY

1. Bann UK *p28*
2. Beluga *p35*
3. Black Bo's (bar *p46*, restaurant *p28*)
4. The Bow Bar *p47*
5. Café Florentin *p36*
6. Café Hub *p37*
7. The Cafeteria *p37*
8. City Café *p39*
9. Creelers *p23*
10. David Bann *p28*
11. The Dial *p29*
12. The Doric Tavern *p30*
13. Dubh Prais *p35*
14. Ecco Vino *p40*
15. EH1 *p40*
16. Elephant House *p40*
17. Favorit *p42*
18. The Forest *p42*
19. The Grain Store *p31*
20. Iguana *p42*
21. La Garrigue *p24*
22. Legume *p24*
23. Le Sept *p25*
24. Maison Bleue *p27*
25. Negociants *p43*
26. North Bridge Brasserie *p31*
27. Old Town Coffee Roasters *p45*
28. Off the Wall *p31*
29. Oxygen Bar & Grill *p45*
30. Plaisir du Chocolat *p45*
31. The Reform *p33*
32. Sandy Bell's *p47*
33. The Tower *p33*
34. Tun Bar & Kitchen *p47*
35. Vermilion *p27*
36. Whistle Binkies *p48*
37. The Witchery by the Castle/The Secret Garden *p34*

The castle rock has probably been fortified since the sixth century AD and by the 12th century there was a route from the Castle in the west to Holyrood Abbey in the east (now ruined). That route is today's Royal Mile and it was around this thoroughfare that the city developed. Until the rich decided to escape to the New Town a couple of centuries ago, this *was* Edinburgh. Today, the Old Town accommodates everything from the Scottish parliament to law courts, while its obvious historical interest means it's the capital's prime attraction for tourists. Consequently, it has a dense concentration of restaurants, café-bars and pubs to serve visitors and locals.

Restaurants

Fish & seafood

Creelers ★

3 Hunter Square (220 4447/www.creelers.co.uk). Bus 35, Nicolson Street-North Bridge buses. **Meals served** noon-2.30pm, 5.30-10.30pm Mon, Thur-Sun; 5.30-10.30pm Tue, Wed. **Average** £££. **Credit** AmEx, MC, V.
This restaurant is the middle sibling in a family of three. The original Creelers is on the Isle of Arran off the Ayrshire coast, while the most recent addition is in

London (Bray Place, Chelsea). They're all owned by Tim and Fran James, and their trademark is fresh, top-quality seafood. (Mr James used to catch the stuff himself.) As you walk in, you'll see a light room with simple wooden tables and a panoramic artwork on one wall; there's more space through the back (non-smoking). The menu offers simple dishes that let the excellence of the raw materials shine through, as well as more elaborate options. So you could start with something as straightforward as langoustine and lemon mayonnaise, but then try home-smoked haddock poached in fennel and thyme cream, with peppered potatoes. Although fish features big, there are always one or two meat and vegetarian options for unpiscivorous diners. Tempting desserts include the likes of pavlova or crème brûlée.

Mediterranean

La Garrigue ★
31 Jeffrey Street (557 3032/www.lagarrigue.co.uk).
Bus 30, 35, Princes Street buses. **Meals served** noon-3pm, 6.30-10pm daily. Closed 1wk Jan. **Average** ££.
Credit AmEx, DC, MC, V.
This restaurant sneaked quietly on to the Edinburgh scene in mid 2001 with little fanfare. Chef-proprietor Jean Michel Gauffre was formerly executive chef at the city's Sheraton Hotel, but La Garrigue allows more scope to pursue his interest in food from his home region: Languedoc in south-east France. The decor is high-class rustic, but the cooking is far from rough and ready and the ingredients are top quality and well sourced. You could start with fish soup or salted cod purée with garlic croûtons and rocket; simplicity is a key feature. Mains include leg of rabbit stuffed with Cevennes ham and juniper berries, and sea bream with chard and tomatoes on Camargue barley. Languedoc wines feature heavily. Obviously, the menu changes, but if you can catch baked figs and blackberries with muscat custard as a dessert, you'll be a happy diner.

Legume
11 South College Street (667 1597). Nicolson Street-North Bridge buses. **Meals served** noon-2pm, 5.30-9.30pm Mon-Sat. **Average** ££. **Credit** AmEx, MC, V.
This French-slanted vegetarian restaurant is hidden up a side street next to Edinburgh University's Old College building. It has the same owners as the rather splendid Off the Wall (*see p31*), and arrived on the scene in 2001. The decor is an economical exercise in good taste: simple, minimal, but homely. By contrast, the food offers all kind of flavours on one plate. To start, you might have lemon

Off the Wall.
See p31.

and mint couscous with tomato confit and roast asparagus. For a main: roast pumpkin and sweet potato cake on a potato and onion rösti, with 'French-style' peas. A typical pudding would be apple parfait with hibiscus sorbet. There's a short but functional wine list, and the service is friendly and efficient. Although Legume is neither loud, nor brash, nor terribly trendy, it's a highly civilised place to pass an evening, with an accomplished standard of cooking.

Le Sept

7 Old Fishmarket Close (225 5428/www.lesept.co.uk). Nicolson Street-North Bridge buses. **Meals served** noon-2pm, 6-10.30pm Mon-Thur; noon-11pm Fri, Sat; 12.30-10pm Sun. **Average** ££. **Credit** AmEx, DC, MC, V.

Few Edinburgh restaurants can beat this one for location. Down a small cobbled street off the Royal Mile, it feels as if it might have been there for centuries. Catch it on a misty night and you're right back with the ghosts of the medieval Old Town. The interior is cellar-like and simple, with arches and wooden tables. The regular menu offers all the starters and mains you'd expect from a French restaurant, and loads of crêpes. Bargain snack? Crêpe, french fries and a glass of house red. There's also an ever-changing seafood menu and a short list of affordable wines. You could start with pan-fried crevettes with white wine, ginger and garlic butter, move on to monkfish

beluga

BELUGA: AWARD-WINNING* BAR & RESTAURANT

beluga is available for private functions and corporate hospitality

for details call **0131 624 4545**

BELUGA BAR & RESTAURANT,
30A CHAMBERS STREET,
EDINBURGH.
T: **0131 624 4545**
E: **belugaenquiries@festival-inns.co.uk**

 www.beluga-edinburgh.com

baked with olives and fresh tarragon, and finish with a crêpe with maple syrup, pecan nuts and ice-cream. There are lighter alternatives.

Maison Bleue

36-38 Victoria Street (226 1900/www.maison-bleue.co.uk). Bus 23, 27, 28, 35, 41, 42, 45. **Meals served** noon-3pm, 5-11pm daily. **Average** ££. **Credit** MC, V.

Forget the French name, Maison Bleue's eclecticism goes way beyond French cooking or even its colonial influences. This is an atmospheric establishment on three floors, with a comfortable bar area, subdued lighting, some bare stone and nice tunes on the CD player. There are no starters and mains as such; the menu is split into 'bouchées', 'brochettes' and 'bouchées doubles'. Bouchées are small (one for a starter, two or three for a full meal): perhaps Vietnamese nems (crispy rice pancakes with fresh crab, shrimp, mint and Chinese greens). Brochettes are char-grilled skewers of chicken, merguez or prawns, or a mixture – all served with harissa couscous and minted yoghurt. Bouchées doubles involve everything from a 10oz steak to duck confit to baked fillet of snapper. Desserts might be pecan pie, chocolate fudge cake or apple tart, and the wine list is two dozen strong (with eight by the glass). Once you're used to the menu structure, you'll love it.

Vermilion ★

Scotsman Hotel, 20 North Bridge (556 5565/ www.thescotsmanhotel.co.uk). Nicolson Street-North Bridge buses. **Meals served** 7-10pm Tue-Sat. **Average** ££££. **Credit** AmEx, DC, MC, V.

Although the terminally swish Scotsman Hotel arrived in 2001, it took until spring 2002 to gets its flagship restaurant open, so Vermilion hasn't had that long to establish itself as serious competition to its elevated peer group (Number One at the Balmoral – *see p62* – is just at the other end of North Bridge, and took six years to achieve Michelin star status). All the same, expectations of excellence rise as diners descend the hotel's grand marble staircase to the dining room, which has the appearance of a contemporary oenological grotto: a subterranean space with walls covered by wine bottles in semi-translucent glass cabinets, subtly back-lit. Three typical courses would be lobster and orange ravioli, ginger jus and honey-roast langoustines to start; sea scallops with caramelised cauliflower risotto and jus of cocoa as a main; and apple tart finé with vanilla ice-cream and cinnamon syrup for dessert. It's already among the very best restaurants in the city, but, like any new kid on the block, trying hard to impress. With a more self-confident rhythm, it could be in the top three.

Gordon's Trattoria (231 High Street, Royal Mile, 225 7992) may be a standard Italian diner, but it's open until midnight most days and 3am on Fridays and Saturdays.

Modern European

Bann UK

*5 Hunter Square (226 1112/www.urbann.co.uk). Bus
35, Nicolson Street-North Bridge buses.* **Meals served**
noon-2.30pm, 6-9pm Mon-Thur; noon-10.30pm Fri-Sun.
Average ££. **Credit** AmEx, DC, MC, V.

These are interesting times at the top end of the
vegetarian restaurant sector in Edinburgh. Bann UK
driving force David Bann departed in 2002 and set up a
new, eponymous restaurant (*see below*), so the one he left
behind has recently made an effort to distinguish itself
from its new rival. Bann UK still does snacks, coffees and
light meals during the day (vegetarian gateau or hot
niçoise-style salad, for example), but the evening menu
now looks a little more formal. To start, the tapas plate
is an accomplished mix of soya bean and pecorino salad,
houmous with olives, chilli stuffed with roast peppers,
capers and mozzarella, and home-made bread. Mock duck
may sound like a bizarre, quasi-Asian main course, but
it has its aficionados. Typical desserts include sticky date
pudding and chocolate tofu mousse. It can get insanely
busy in August during the Festival.

Black Bo's

*57-61 Blackfriars Street (557 6136). Bus 35, Nicolson
Street-North Bridge buses.* **Meals served** 6-10.30pm
Wed, Thur; noon-2pm, 6-10.30pm Fri, Sat. **Average** ££.
Credit MC, V.

Is this the only vegetarian restaurant in the world that
sells meat? For years, Black Bo's fought it out with Bann
UK (*see above*) for the title of best European-style veggie
restaurant in the city – that was before the arrival of
Legume (*see p24*) and David Bann (*see below*). Then in
early 2003 it bowed to 'customer demand' and introduced
a few meat and fish dishes. Now, as you sit in its simple
wooden bistro surroundings, lit by candles and with good
modern tunes on the sound system, you can choose the
likes of sirloin steak with rosemary and green ginger
wine sauce. Vegetarian or not, Black Bo's trademark is
still a tremendous sense of adventure with fruit – which
diners tend to love or loathe. Baked pineapple with chilli
and figs, flambéed with dark rum, would serve as a
starter; pepper stuffed with pistachio and cumin soufflé,
with lime yoghurt, is a typical main. Which makes a pud
like strawberry cheesecake seem low-key. Next door is a
loveable bar with the same name (*see p46*).

David Bann ★

*56-58 St Mary's Street (556 5888/www.davidbann.com).
Bus 7, 14, 33, 35, 37.* **Meals served** 11am-1am daily.
Average ££. **Credit** AmEx, MC, V.

The **Royal Museum** (Chambers Street, 225 7534) has a reasonable coffee bar, which often seems lost in the corner of a vast and impressive 'bird-cage' atrium dating from 1888.

David Bann split from Bann UK (*see above*) and started up his own place in St Mary's Street in late 2002. Both are vegetarian and even look similar (minimal and tasteful, with dark wood fittings and dark red decor). After a few early teething troubles, the restaurant has developed a deft touch in the kitchen and smooth service. You can choose from starters and snacks (dim sum, soup of the day), light meals, salads, mains and sides. Three courses could entail aloo bonda (spiced potato dumplings with coconut and coriander sauce and spicy tomato salsa), gorgonzola polenta with roast Mediterranean vegetables and a sweet tomato salad, then amaretto cheesecake. There are appropriate wines, good beers (Fraoch heather ale, organic lagers from Germany) and the only caveat is that this site has seen the death of a procession of restaurants over the past few years – hopefully, David Bann can stay the course.

The Dial

44-46 George IV Bridge (225 7179). Bus 23, 27, 28, 41, 42, 45. **Meals served** noon-3pm, 6-10.30pm daily. **Average** ££. **Credit** AmEx, MC, V.

The Dial is a popular restaurant, but could almost be a secret club. The main dining area is one level below

Ecco Vino. *See p40.*

The Tower. *See p33.*

George IV Bridge and surprisingly easy to miss (a shopfront entrance allows access via a steep flight of stairs). Once inside, it feels spacious and light, with blonde wood and pastel colours. Typical starters include trout fish cakes, salmon, duck or a soup of the day such as wild mushroom, garlic and white wine. Mains can feature pigeon marinated in teriyaki on celeriac; monkfish and prawns with red pepper vinaigrette; and camembert-glazed Aberdeen Angus, with port jus. The dessert list carries items like apple and cinnamon crumble and Belgian chocolate tart. Service walks the line between informal and efficient, but it's friendly, and the wine list has all you'll need. Nice candlelight in the evenings.

The Doric Tavern

15-16 Market Street (225 1084/www.thedoric.co.uk).
Bus 23, 27, 28, 41, 42, 45. **Meals served** noon-11pm daily. **Average** ££. **Credit** AmEx, DC, MC, V.
This slightly cramped restaurant and wine bar behind Waverley Station is an almost bohemian establishment. Reached up a flight of stairs, it's all very old-wood with art noodlings playing a big role in the bar decor. The adjacent dining room has an open kitchen, with the menu and wines sketched up on blackboards. You could start with sole and asparagus terrine with lemon and dill vinaigrette, followed by char-grilled cod with pineapple salsa and sour cream, then date sponge with butterscotch sauce. It's the kind of place students bring their parents,

and can be faintly boisterous; its popularity endures despite a potential scattiness about service when it's full. If you don't want to eat, the bar is a great place to spend an indolent afternoon with a bottle of wine.

The Grain Store

30 Victoria Street (225 7635/www.grainstore-restaurant. co.uk). Bus 11, 23, 41, 42, 45. **Meals served** noon-2pm, 6-10pm Mon-Thur; noon-3pm, 6-11pm Fri-Sun. **Average** £££. **Credit** AmEx, MC, V.

A firm local favourite, tucked away upstairs off a winding Old Town street, the Grain Store is nothing like the vegetarian zealot its name might suggest. There are a few candelit recesses that come into their own during the evening, but this establishment has always seemed to excel as a place to while away an afternoon by a window, after lunch, and after a bottle or two of wine. For that lunch you can do a tapas-style pick 'n' mix with small dishes (toasted goat's cheese and hazelnuts, a single Loch Fyne oyster, for example) or have a proper main course, such as haunch of venison with celeriac purée, gin and juniper berries. A full-on three-course dinner could involve duck rillette salad, then guinea fowl with oyster mushrooms and cured pork, finished off with meringue and praline ice-cream. Some nice wines too.

North Bridge Brasserie

Scotsman Hotel, 20 North Bridge (556 5565/ www.thescotsmanhotel.co.uk). Nicolson Street-North Bridge buses. **Meals served** 12.15-2.30pm, 6.15-10pm Mon-Thur, Sun; 12.15-2.30pm, 6.15-10.30pm Sat. **Average** £££. **Credit** AmEx, MC, V.

Housed in the former offices of the Scotsman newspaper, this upmarket hotel opened for business in 2001. Its brasserie faces, eponymously, on to North Bridge and looks as grandiose and eclectic as only an Edwardian foyer, updated with modern fittings, possibly can. There is a high ceiling, a central staircase and tables at floor and balcony level. The menu is highly flexible, with starters, assorted salads, vegetarian mains, grills and puddings. So if you just want a large salad of corn-fed chicken with orange, and a glass of wine, that's fine. On the other hand, you could try half a dozen oysters, followed by grilled tiger prawns, parmesan mash on the side, then white chocolate custard cup to finish. There's a definite buzz to the brasserie; the big sister restaurant in the hotel, Vermilion (*see p27*), is somewhat more chichi.

Off The Wall ★

105 High Street (558 1497/www.off-the-wall.co.uk). Bus 35, Nicolson Street-North Bridge buses. **Meals served** noon-2pm, 6-10pm Mon-Sat. **Average** ££££. **Credit** AmEx, MC, V.

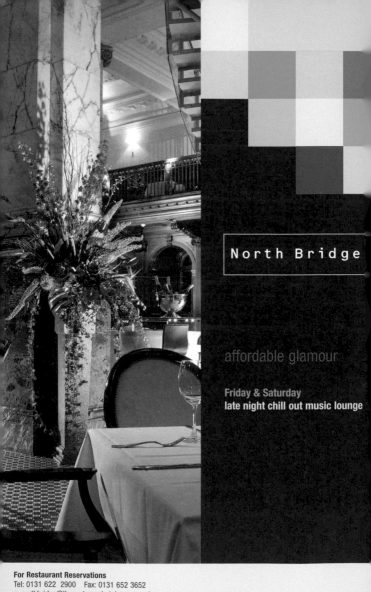

North Bridge

affordable glamour

**Friday & Saturday
late night chill out music lounge**

For Restaurant Reservations
Tel: 0131 622 2900   Fax: 0131 652 3652
e: northbridge@thescotsmanhotelgroup.co.uk

North Bridge Brasserie
20 North Bridge   Edinburgh   EH1 1YT

From the moment the waitress brings an amuse-bouche of cream of cauliflower soup with truffle oil until the last impressions of mango and almond tart ebb from the palate, this establishment keeps its diners pretty much content. Set up by David Anderson (chef) and Aileen Wilson (front of house) in South College Street in 1997, it moved to Edinburgh's main tourist drag in 2000. Up one flight of stairs, Off The Wall is a haven of quietly tasteful decor and fine cooking completely at odds with its tartan shop neighbours. (In August, it's a particularly civilised escape from the Festival chaos outside.) A starter of tuna on puy lentil and sweet pepper salad energises the most jaded customer, while a main such as seared sea bass on fennel and spinach with lemon butter sauce is virtually symphonic. Rabbit, pigeon, veal, venison and good old Scotch beef also feature.

The Reform

267 Canongate (558 9992/www.reformrestaurant.com). *Bus 30, 35.* **Meals served** noon-2.30pm, 6-10.30pm daily. **Average** £££. **Credit** AmEx, MC, V.
The Reform is in the heart of Edinburgh tourist country and for many years it catered self-consciously to that trade (always something meaty with Arran mustard sauce on the menu, for instance). Then in 2000, along came a new manager, a new chef, contemporary decor and it went fusion – a definite improvement. Now diners can have starters as diverse as ginger-marinated tofu with roast vegetables and ricotta in filo roll, or Thai broth with coriander dumplings. Elaborate mains include plum wine-marinated kangaroo rump (on quince and cinnamon tart, of course), and Moroccan spiced salmon fillet. Desserts, oddly enough, can be as simple as brandy and sultana cake ice-cream – spectacularly presented. So don't let the exterior of the restaurant affect your judgement – it may appear a tad traditional, but it's far from that. Service is fine, and the wine list affordable if short. A refuge from the tartan nonsense of the Royal Mile.

The Tower ★

Museum of Scotland, Chambers Street (225 3003/ *www.tower-restaurant.com).* *Bus 23, 27, 28, 41, 42, 45.* **Meals served** noon-11pm daily. **Average** £££. **Credit** AmEx, DC, MC, V.
There are few restaurants anywhere with a more impressive setting. The Tower is on the top floor of the Museum of Scotland, a repository of Caledonian culture that opened in late 1998. The views over the Old Town can transport you back in time, while the chic interior wouldn't look out of place in a bigger capital city. Service is deft and the wine list affordable – but with some star bins for those looking to blow serious money. The menu

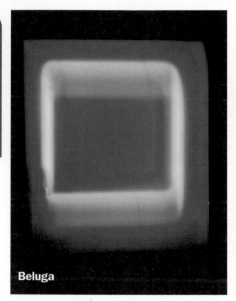

Beluga

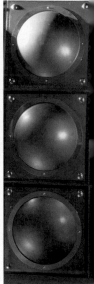

is flexible (have a salad and side dish if you like), with a trenchantly British feel in places, as well as smart international flourishes. A starter like smoked onion soup with parsley dumplings is warming; lobster claw with pickled vegetables more of a departure. Mains can be as traditional as fish and chips with pea purée, or a little more contemporary: seared salmon with lemongrass, chilli and coconut risotto. For dessert, try the elderflower and pickled ginger crème brûlée.

The Witchery by the Castle/
The Secret Garden ★
Castlehill (225 5613/www.thewitchery.com). Bus 27, 28, 35, 41, 42, 45. **Meals served** noon-4pm, 5.30-11.30pm daily. **Average** ££££. **Credit** AmEx, DC, MC. V.
Edinburgh doesn't have that many destination restaurants, so it would be remiss not to mention these two as they certainly qualify on the basis of location, reputation and as an attraction for visiting celebs. Often referred to as just 'the Witchery', we're actually talking about two dining rooms: the Witchery itself is a high-class, leathery/wooden establishment just yards from Edinburgh Castle Esplanade, while the adjacent Secret

Garden oozes even more atmosphere (tapestries, arched windows, candles) and is very popular for major romantic occasions. Both have the same menu, and awesome wine list, which runs to more than 130 pages. A typical meal might involve roast mallard breast to start, pan-roasted monkfish as a main, and white peach tarte tatin for dessert. In recent years it hasn't always delivered at the giddy heights you'd expect, and it is very expensive – although brilliant when on form. For an economical look-see, try the bargain lunch or theatre supper.

Scottish

Dubh Prais

123B High Street (557 5732/www.bencraighouse.co.uk). Bus 35, Nicolson Street-North Bridge buses. **Meals served** noon-2pm, 6.30-10.30pm Tue-Fri; 6.30-10pm Sat. Closed 1wk Jan, 1wk Mar, 1wk Oct. **Average** ££. **Credit** AmEx, MC, V.

A long-established fixture in the middle of Edinburgh's tourist strip, Dubh Prais (pronounced 'doo prah', it means 'the black pot') takes Scottish ingredients and actually does something quite deft with them. A three-course dinner in its small basement space could involve mixed seafood soup or smoked salmon and pickled scallop salad to start, followed by breast of chicken stuffed with Dunsyre Blue cheese (from Lanarkshire) with sherry sauce, or saddle of venison in beetroot sauce with guinea fowl fritters. Atholl Brose parfait makes a fine dessert. (Atholl Brose itself is usually made from cream, Drambuie, almonds and oatmeal.) Given the skill of the kitchen, this restaurant certainly appeals to visitors (who are wowed by the Scottishness), but locals too.

Café-bars & Cafés

The **Scotch Whisky Heritage Centre** (354 Castlehill, Royal Mile, 220 0441, www.whisky-heritage.co.uk) may be a bit Disneyish for some tastes, but it does tell the story of Scotch.

Beluga

30A Chambers Street (624 4545). Nicolson Street-North Bridge buses. **Open** 9am-1am daily. **Meals served** *Bar* noon-10pm daily. *Restaurant* noon-2.30pm, 6-10pm Mon-Thur, Sun; noon-2.30pm, 6-10.30pm Fri, Sat. **Average** £££. **Credit** AmEx, MC, V.

This fairly cavernous basement style-bar-with-food, and an attached restaurant one floor up, is located in what used to be the city's dental hospital. On weekend nights, the bar is packed with a twentysomething crowd (boys in Ben Sherman, girls in backless tops), high on music, atmosphere and dating hormones. But when quieter, it can be a relaxed and roomy place to enjoy a light meal – pork with sage and apple sausages and creamy mash, or

Festival fever

Ask a local cynic about eating or drinking in Edinburgh during August and they might simply say, 'Don't come'. This is primetime. Aside from all the usual visitors who arrive at the height of summer to see the Castle, the Royal Mile, the Palace of Holyroodhouse and other attractions, the assorted arts festivals being held in the city crank up the numbers to ludicrous levels. It's been claimed that the population doubles or even trebles.

But backtrack a moment. Assorted arts festivals? Indeed. Although many people refer to 'the Edinburgh Festival' as if it was just one big jamboree, there are actually six administratively separate but overlapping events: the **International Festival** (the main one with classical music, theatre, ballet and more); the **Fringe** (in existence since the late 1940s as an alternative to the International Festival with much comedy, music and student noodling); the **International Film Festival** (self-explanatory); the **Jazz and Blues Festival** (ditto); the **International Book Festival** (ditto again); and the **Military Tattoo** (displays of martial and musical prowess at the Castle Esplanade). Full details on www.edinburgh-festivals.com.

aubergine and goat's cheese ravioli. Or, indeed, just a coffee. The upstairs restaurant aims for a Scottish-Pacific Rim crossover, and seems to be finding its feet with time. A typical three-course meal might entail pan-seared, whisky-marinated salmon with Asian greens to start, grilled lamb loin with mushroom risotto as a main, and raspberry and white chocolate mousse for pudding.

Café Florentin
8 St Giles Street (225 6267). Bus 23, 27, 28, 41, 42, 45.
Open 8am-6pm Mon-Sat. **No credit cards**.
Just off the Royal Mile by St Giles Cathedral, with a sunflower logo, yellow walls and wooden tables, Café Florentin is a prime spot for tourists and Fringe-goers to stop off for a blast of coffee and pastries, or a savoury snack. Options include good fruit tarts, waffles, filled croissants, ciabattas, soups, and salads. It's not exclusively touristy; you'll also find students, and assorted legal types from the nearby law courts. There are two small rooms downstairs and a more extensive upstairs space that may be closed during winter when it's quiet, but will certainly be open at the height of the season (Easter to the end of August). Florentin can get very busy, especially during the Festival.

All this talent means the audiences are wildly mixed (everything from packs of twentysomethings seeking lager and laughter to wealthy retired Americans seeking high art and authentic Scottish cuisine). The consequence is that everywhere obvious to eat or drink is packed, especially around the Royal Mile, from the upmarket **Witchery by the Castle** (*see p34*) to the likes of the **City Café** (*see p39*) or **EH1** (*see p40*). You have been warned.

On the plus side, many establishments extend their opening hours, and odd café-bars and drinking dens are set up in Fringe venues, just for a few weeks, to deal with demand. The **Assembly Rooms** (54 George Street, New Town) or the **Pleasance Theatre** (60 The Pleasance, South) are two of the busiest. Then there is a range of arts venues with bars and cafés where you can just embrace a festival experience of whatever type, and launch into the melee; the **Traverse Theatre Bar**, the **Filmhouse Bar** (for both, *see p128*) and **Café Hub** (*see p37*) are all real nerve centres. By contrast, if you want some peace, this might be time to head for the real fringe – and try Glasgow.

Café Hub

Castlehill (473 2067). Bus 23, 27, 28, 35, 41, 42, 45.
Open 9.30am-6pm Mon, Sun; 9.30am-10pm Tue-Sat.
Meals served 9.30am-9.30pm daily. **Average** ££.
Credit AmEx, DC, MC, V.

The Hub opened in 1999 as the headquarters for the Edinburgh International Festival. Completed in 1845, the building was originally an assembly hall and offices for the Church of Scotland; although the café only occupies part of the space, it's still fairly cavernous. The flexible daytime menu means you could have just a coffee and a sandwich or a glass of wine and a light meal. Sit in or out – there's a terrace. The evening menu might offer barley risotto cake with spinach and smoked cheese to start; loin of venison with pancetta and wild mushrooms as a main; and baked apricot brioche with orange cream for dessert. During any August lunchtime, this can be the busiest place in the whole city. On a quiet winter's evening, the lack of fellow diners makes whispering de rigueur.

Fed up with expensive restaurants and designer café-bars? Head instead for the good old **Baked Potato Shop** (56 Cockburn Street, 225 7572).

The Cafeteria

Fruitmarket Gallery, 45 Market Street (226 1843/ www.fruitmarket.co.uk/cafe.html). Princes Street buses.
Open 11am-5pm Mon-Sat; noon-5pm Sun. **Meals served** noon-4pm daily. **Credit** MC, V.

Fresh danish pastries keep the mid-morning grazers happy and there is always a selection of gateaux for the more leisurely afternoon browser, but it's lunchtime that sees the real action in the café of the Fruitmarket, possibly Edinburgh's hippest public art gallery. Staff aim to fill up customers with big baguette melts, salads and pasta dishes, all washed down with wine or a bottle of Beck's. The gallery can have pretty challenging exhibitions, so you might need the big portions for mental energy. As with most other arts venues in the city, it gets pretty busy in August during the Festival.

City Café ★

19 Blair Street (220 0125). Nicolson Street-North Bridge buses. **Open** 11am-1am daily. **Meals served** 11am-11pm Mon-Thur; 11am-10pm Fri-Sun. **Credit** MC, V.

As much a part of Edinburgh as the Castle, although not quite as old, the City Café has the look of a 1950s diner, has a downstairs DJ space and a pool table, serves all-day breakfasts, caters to the pre-club crowd later on – and there's even a small aquarium if it's got all too much and you just want to stare at fish. The food is fill-you-up stuff: pasta, nachos, paninis. House burgers include lamb and rosemary with fries and salad, while the all-day breakfasts (carnivore and vegetarian versions) really kick-start your morning (or afternoon or evening). Bottled

The best viewpoints

Elephant House
A 17th-century atmosphere as you look out from the back room to Greyfriars churchyard and beyond. *See p40*.

Harvey Nichols Forth Floor
Nice panorama from top shop's eaterie, east city centre. *See p58*.

Oloroso
Nice panorama from top restaurant, west city centre. *See p62*.

Old Chain Pier
A pub virtually in the Firth of Forth; next stop Fife. *See p94*.

The Tower
Classic views from the roof of the Museum of Scotland. There's also a terrace. *See p33*.

lagers include Budvar and Furstenberg, and a bottle of wine won't break the bank. Altogether an Edinburgh classic – and can you spot the legendary spelling error behind the bar?

Ecco Vino ★

19 Cockburn Street (225 1441). Bus 35, Nicolson Street-North Bridge buses. **Open** noon-midnight Mon-Fri, Sun; noon-1am Sat. **Meals served** noon-10pm daily. **Average** £. **Credit** AmEx, MC, V.

The formula is so simple, it's genius. Create a basic Italian menu with some straightforward dishes and the odd daily special (chorizo and roast tomato pasta, say). Create an Italian-slanted wine list. Store your wines up on one wall as a design feature above the tables, run the bar along the other side of the room, choose predominantly wooden decor, light candles, wait for clientele. And since it opened in autumn 2001, the clientele has come. Ecco Vino is between the Royal Mile and Waverley Station in prime tourist country, but it's the opposite of a tourist trap. All the wines are available by the bottle or glass, the vibe is relaxed and quite atmospheric. The food can be as simple and snackish as olives and bread, or as filling as spinach and nutmeg frittata with a side order of garlic bread topped by good-quality mozzarella.

EH1

197 High Street (220 5277). Bus 35, Nicolson Street-North Bridge buses. **Open** 9am-1am daily. **Meals served** 9am-7pm daily. **Average** £. **Credit** AmEx, MC, V.

On a fine sunny day in August there's no better place than EH1 to sit outside and watch the chaos of the Fringe festival. The Royal Mile is pedestrianised at that time of year, and numerous performers will be doing impromptu street theatre; relax and take it all in with a snack and an ice-cold Czech Budvar or a glass of wine. The typical café-bar fare includes small dishes, wraps, burgers, pasta, salads, sandwiches – and more. That means breakfast (vegetarian or traditional), nachos with mozzarella and stuffed jalapenos, venison burger with fries or pasta with salmon, leeks and chives. The best tables are the ones through the back, overlooking Cockburn Street.

Elephant House

21 George IV Bridge (220 5355/www.elephant-house. co.uk). Bus 23, 27, 28, 41, 42, 45. **Open** 8am-10pm Mon-Fri; 9am-11pm Sat, Sun. **Average** £. **Credit** MC, V.

This very popular and busy café not far from the university has a vaguely ethnic look and a fetish for pachyderms. The clientele includes tea-sipping students, lecturers having a panini while they read the newspaper, and grandmothers buying their grandkids a cake before they visit the nearby Museum of Scotland. The Elephant

House is so established these days that it even has its own merchandise (T-shirts, postcards), but the victuals on offer are pretty good. Some of the teas and coffees are first-rate (and organic), there's a choice of eight wines (all at £8.95 a bottle) and food choices include salads, baguettes and savouries such as mushroom and jarlsberg quiche or ricotta and spinach pie. The main room through the back has some great Old Town views.

Branch: **Elephant & Bagels** 37 Marshall Street, Nicolson Square, South (668 4404).

Favorit

19-20 Teviot Place (220 6880). Bus 1, 7, 14, 22, 25, 35, 49. **Open** 8am-3am daily. **Credit** AmEx, DC, MC, V.

With its long opening hours, Favorit provides everything from breakfast for workers in a hurry to nightcaps for clapped-out clubbers. The sandwiches have a distinctly American flavour; pastrami and gruyère on rye is typical. It also acts as a deli and gadget shop, so if you drop in for a smoothie, don't be too surprised if you walk out with a new espresso machine. Decor-wise, it's Americana-land with a definite diner feel. Somehow the Teviot Place branch feels more snack 'n' go while the Leven Street one invites you to linger.

Branch: 30-32 Leven Street, South (221 1800).

The Forest

9 West Port, Grassmarket (221 0237/www.theforest. org.uk). Bus 2. **Open** noon-11pm daily. **No credit cards**.

The Forest is a 'community-volunteer-run event and information space artists collective' kind of affair with evening discussions, movies and similar – so no surprise that it's near the local art college. The look is scruffy, with squishy sofas to sink into, while the food includes tortilla wraps, falafels, quiche, hearty soups, salads and veggie burgers. It seems to be staffed and populated by ethereal young women and earnest young men; if you popped in wearing a suit, with the *FT* under your arm, heads would turn.

Iguana

41 Lothian Street (220 4288/www.iguanaedinburgh. co.uk). Nicolson Street-North Bridge buses. **Open** 9am-1am daily. **Meals served** 9am-10pm daily. **Average** ££. **Credit** AmEx, MC, V.

Given its proximity to Edinburgh University (literally across the road), the Iguana thrives as a place to dawdle with coffee during the day; it gets a lot jiggier in the evenings when DJs appear and the sound level is upped a notch or two (Wednesday to Sunday). The environment is style bar rustic – chunky wooden tables and metal twiddles – while the food is all things to all people. There's a good cooked breakfast, sandwiches and wraps

(hot beef with grain mustard), small dishes (chicken skewers with satay sauce), pasta, noodles and other main dishes (cajun beer and potato goulash). In Scotland's brief summer, you can even sit outside.

Negociants

45 Lothian Street (225 6313). Nicolson Street-North Bridge buses. **Open** 9am-3am Mon-Sat; 10am-3pm Sun. **Meals served** 10am-10pm daily. **Average ££. Credit** MC, V.

If you ever want to hide in a café-bar until the small hours of the morning, nibbling nachos and drinking artisan beer from Belgium or cheap house wine, this is the place. Negociants seems to have been around forever. As the name suggests, it has a vaguely French feel; it's also spacious, with lots of mirrors and big windows looking out towards the university buildings opposite. Don't be in a hurry though, as the pedestrian service is legendary. You can have coffee and a croissant during the day, but there's also an extensive menu offering everything from a full cooked breakfast to fajitas, pasta and main dishes such as grilled smoked haddock with prawns, stir-fried vegetables and hollandaise. At night, it's snacks only. Like the Iguana next door (*see above*) you can sit outside in summer. Downstairs is the technically separate club-

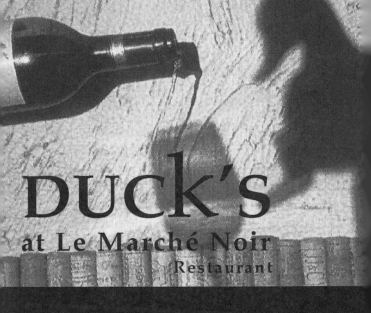

DUCK'S
at Le Marché Noir
Restaurant

With one of the most comprehensive wine lists in the country and a cooking professionalism rated by all the major guides, it is easy to se why Duck's at Le Marché Noir has been at the top for over 11 years.

Duck's boasts an intimate and relaxed atmosphere, with its tradema white linen tables and softly glowing candles. Locally sourced produ is cooked respectfully, under the influence of our international team of chefs.

Both rooms are regularly hired - either individually or together - for private parties, receptions, corporate luncheons or dinners, and othe such special occasions. The staff at Duck's are able to offer help with anything from menus, pipers or Whisky tastings, to hotel or B&B accommodation, Edinburgh events and other local information.

2/4 Eyre Place, Edinburgh EH3 5E
0131 558 160
bookings@ducks.co.uk   www.ducks.co.u
Proprietor - Malcolm Duc

bar, Medina, with an attractive harem-decadence theme and space for dancing – if you're not too busy reclining on an intricately patterned cushion.

Old Town Coffee Roasters

32 Victoria Street (225 7497/www.ijmellischeesemonger. com). Bus 23, 27, 28, 35, 41, 42, 45. **Open** 10am-6pm Mon-Sat. **Credit** MC, V.

Iain J Mellis is an acclaimed cheesemonger; some say the best in the UK. His original shop at 30A Victoria Street sells some of the finest and most interesting UK and Irish artisan cheeses available, and their popularity has seen his empire spread to another two branches in the capital and one in Glasgow. Next door to that first shop is this tiny deli and café. There is a very small bar to sit at on the ground floor, and a couple of tables up one flight of stairs that overlook the counter. The coffee is excellent, there's assorted antipasti and sandwiches (good charcuterie for a cheese specialist), but the big seller is that if an obscure cheese from next door takes your fancy, you can have it in a sandwich or on a platter. By definition then, the best cheese sarnies in Scotland.

Branches: IJ Mellis Cheesemonger 30A Victoria Street, Old Town (226 6215); 205 Bruntsfield Place, South (447 8889); 6 Bakers Place, New Town & Stockbridge (225 6566).

Oxygen Bar & Grill

3-5 Infirmary Street (557 9997/www.oxygen-edinburgh. co.uk). Nicolson Street-North Bridge buses. **Open** 10am-1am Mon-Sat; noon-1am Sun. **Meals served** 11am-9pm Mon-Sat; noon-9pm Sun. **Average** £. **Credit** MC, V.

Oxygen opened with a flourish at the end of 1999 as the only establishment in Edinburgh to sell canisters of oxygen. As a gimmick, it was short-lived (pure oxygen, drinking and cigarette lighters don't mix). Despite looking a little less bright than it used to, this style bar has endured thanks to its proximity to the university and the club-packed Cowgate. Food-wise, expect pasta, noodles and sandwiches as well as light bites (peppered tuna with roast capiscum or asparagus and mushroom risotto) and more substantial 'plates' (braised venison sausages on mash or a wrap of wasabi chicken, spring onion and crème fraîche). Enjoy an eclectic snack or iridescent pitcher of cocktail before heading off clubbing.

Plaisir du Chocolat ★

251-253 Canongate (556 9524). Bus 30, 35. **Open** 10am-6pm Wed-Sun. **Meals served** 10am-5pm Wed-Sun. **Average** ££. **Credit** AmEx, MC, V.

This opened in summer 2000 and instantly gained a reputation as one of the best cafés in the city. It's a salon with the biggest list of teas in Christendom and hot chocolate concoctions that make women weep with joy and quasi-sexual delight. There's also a good kitchen; the French savouries (spinach and goat's cheese tart, perhaps, or a Mediterranean platter) are highly accomplished. You can have a very fulfilling lunch with some decent wine, but hot choc junkies will simply expire with pleasure affecting a When Sally Met Couverture scene ('uuuh, uuuh, oooh, aaaargh…'). If you're Harry, galvanise yourself for embarrassment. Definitely not a place for lager and crisps, incidentally.

Pubs & Bars

Black Bo's

57-61 Blackfriars Street (557 6136). Bus 35, Nicolson Street-North Bridge buses. **Open** 4pm-1am daily.
No credit cards.

Adjacent to its namesake restaurant (*see p28*), Black Bo's is an appealing scruff of an establishment that looks as if it was shoehorned into a space that was never meant to be a bar. There's a motley collection of furniture, club posters and the whole place is festooned with fairylights that look as if they went up one Christmas and never came down. Not a draught ale pub (Staropramen or

Whistle Binkies.
See p48.

Grolsch on tap is about as interesting as it gets), it does offer some good single malt whiskies, but atmosphere and attitude mark it out rather than the drinks choice. Downstairs, there's a tiny pool room that looks as if it was hewn from the very rock of the Old Town.

The Bow Bar ★

80 West Bow (226 7667). Bus 23, 27, 28, 41, 45. **Open** noon-11.30pm Mon-Sat; noon-11pm Sun. **Credit** MC, V.

It's not big, but it is clever. The Bow Bar offers one of the largest range of whiskies of any pub in the city – more than you can count – and backs this up with a selection of Scottish and English cask ales that includes rarities only real enthusiasts would have encountered before (Bitter and Twisted from Dollar, Thrappledouser from Perth, Black Cuillin from Skye). The decor is basic, with wooden fittings, chairs and leather bench seats. When it's busy, you'll be lucky to find anywhere to park your backside, but with an excellent pint and a rare single malt chaser, who cares?

Sandy Bell's

25 Forrest Road (225 2751). Bus 35, Nicolson Street-North Bridge buses. **Open** noon-12.45am Mon-Sat; noon-11pm Sun. **No credit cards**.

No frills in Sandy Bell's, just a space for drink and music. There's a folk session every weeknight, which picks up from around 9pm, and also on weekend afternoons. Local musicians come to play Scottish folk tunes together, an activity that's fairly rare these days in Edinburgh pubs. You get the general gist of the place from the bust above the bar of Hamish Henderson (cultural hero; the man who wrote 'Freedom Come All Ye', which many swear would make a much better national anthem than 'Flower of Scotland'). Draught ales include Deuchars IPA and Directors Bitter, and there'a a fair choice of whisky too.

Tun Bar & Kitchen

Holyrood Road (557 9297). Bus 64. **Open** 11am-11pm Mon-Thur; 11am-midnight Fri, Sat; 11am-7pm Sun. **Credit** AmEx, DC, MC, V.

One day there will be a Scottish parliament at the foot of Holyrood Road – when the contractors finally finish and the elected representatives move in. Meanwhile, developments have gone up around the area in anticipation, this glass-fronted, multi-use building (formerly part of a brewery), which houses the BBC, the Commission for Racial Equality and others. On the ground floor is the Tun (spacious, contemporary in style), where politicians, journalists, lobbyists and others will one day meet and mingle. The wine's cheap (all under £12 a bottle) and there's a selection of cocktails with silly names and sillier ingredients. It's also adjacent to

The **Edinburgh Literary Pub Tour** is a rolling piece of performance art that has been mingling beer and Scottish literary history since 1996. Call 226 6665 or check http://home. btconnect.com/ sltc

Holyrood Park and close to the tourist attraction of Dynamic Earth. (There's food too, but it's delivered by the most irritating system ever devised. You order and pay at the bar, and are given an alarm gizmo that activates when your meal is ready; you then have to go to a servery to collect it.)

Whistle Binkies

6 Niddry Street (557 5114/www.whistlebinkies.com). Nicolson Street-North Bridge buses. **Open** 7pm-3am daily. **Credit** MC, V.

This is Edinburgh's late-night, pub-rock hangout par excellence. It doesn't even open until mid evening, but then stays awake until 3am, and there's always some sort of live band. That would be an actual band doing rock, indie, soul, funk, blues, ska, Latino (or just covers) rather than a DJ. Over the years, it built up a reputation as a real grungey cellar, then a major refurb in winter 2002/03 spruced up the place considerably – though it still has a stone floor and that subterranean feel. It has a few cask ales (Caledonian 80/-, Deuchars IPA, Raven Ale from Orkney) and cellar-like alcoves off the main bar area. There's also an entrance on South Bridge.

The best style bars

The beautiful people...

Rick's (*see p68*) and the **Opal Lounge** (*see p67*) function as cosmopolitan arbiters of taste for the aspirational, but **Oloroso** (*see p62*) is for the honeys with the money.

Shaken, not stirred...

For proper cocktails – rather than your Screaming Orgasm nonsense – head to **Rogue** (*see p126*), downstairs at **Hurricane** (*see p59*), the **North Bridge Brasserie** (*see p31*) or **blue bar-café** (*see p127*).

Hey, baby

For the under-30 mass dating crowd, **Beluga** (*see p35*) has more designer labels, while **Medina** (downstairs at **Negociants**; *see p43*) has the students and beautiful Eurotrash.

Flat-out fun

If enjoyment is more important than narcissism, try the **Basement** (*see p88*), **Montpeliers** (*see p113*) or **Bar Sirius** (*see p88*).

Edinburgh:
New Town
& Stockbridge

MAP KEY

A 'new town' was first discussed in the mid 18th century and completed in the 19th; an escape from the squalor of medieval Edinburgh, around the Royal Mile, for those who could afford to live in elegant Georgian terraces. The blocks between Princes Street (its southern boundary) and Queen Street are bustling with shops, offices, restaurants and bars. Once north of Queen Street Gardens, though, the New Town's real character kicks in; it's quiet, largely residental and oozes old money – with most pubs and dining opportunities on main thoroughfares like Dundas Street and Howe Street. Meanwhile, Stockbridge, to the north-west, has a character – and eating and drinking choices – all of its own.

Restaurants

American

Bell's Diner

7 St Stephen Street (225 8116). Bus 19A, 24, 28. **Open** 6-10.30pm Mon-Fri, Sun; noon-10.30pm Sat. **Average** £. **Credit** MC, V.

This tiny, unadorned eaterie in the heart of Stockbridge has been around since 1972. There are two reasons for such unusual longevity: first, the burgers and steaks that form the bulk of the menu are pretty good; second, even

if customers drift away to other restaurants, or even other cities, Bell's Diner is still there when they drift back. Those celebrated burgers come in 4oz, 6oz and 8oz sizes (fries and salad on the side) with various toppings like roquefort or pepper. Vegetarians get the best nutburger in the city. Fresh salads serve nicely as starters, while pancakes with peaches and cream is a typical pudding. The house wines, chalked up on a blackboard, are pretty affordable. After more than 30 years, why change a winning formula?

Asian

Loon Fung

2 Warriston Place (556 1781). Bus 23, 27, 36. **Meals served** noon-midnight Mon-Fri; 2pm-midnight Sat, Sun. **Average** ££. **Credit** AmEx, MC, V.

Down on Canonmills and handily placed for the Botanic Gardens, Loon Fung is one of Edinburgh's better Cantonese restaurants; the kind that Sino-Scots describe as a cut above. The decor is nothing to write home about, but there's a great selection of dim sum, and specials include baked crab in ginger sauce and steamed chicken with mushrooms. Often busy when everywhere else is deserted, it's been a stalwart of the scene for longer than anyone remembers, and diners who haven't been for

Opal Lounge. *See p67.*

years still talk about such legendary dishes as lemon chicken or crispy duck with pancakes. If the Loon Fung was in your neighbourhood, you'd be a happy citizen.

Siam Erawan

48 Howe Street (226 3675). Bus 13, 19A, 24, 28. **Meals served** noon-2.30pm, 6-10.45pm Mon-Sat; 6-10.45pm Sun. **Average** ££. **Credit** AmEx, MC, V.

Sitting in a New Town basement at the corner of Howe Street and North West Circus Place, Siam Erawan is a neat and polite establishment that has been around for more than ten years – a long time compared to other Thai restaurants in the city. It's doing something right, then? Quite. The mixed starter selection is a good introduction (fish cakes, chicken satay, pork ribs, prawn tempura and steamed prawn and crabmeat parcels). The rest of the menu has a range of larger satays, soups, salads, seafood, curries, a decent vegetarian selection and more. Duck features strongly (pad gium chai, for example: sweet and sour duck stir-fry with mustard greens), and there's also an effort to use local ingredients in dishes like marinated and char-grilled Scottish sirloin, served with sticky rice and tamarind sauce, and pan-fried Scottish salmon topped with penang sauce. Nice coconut ice-cream too. **Branches: Erawan Oriental** 14 South St Andrew Street, New Town & Stockbridge (556 4242); **Erawan Express** 176 Rose Street, New Town & Stockbridge (220 0059).

L'Alba d'Oro at 5 Henderson Row (557 2580) is the best fish and chip shop in Edinburgh bar none.

Yo! Sushi/Yo! Below

66 Rose Street (220 6040/www.yosushi.com). Princes Street buses. **Open** *Yo! Below* 5.30pm-1am Mon-Thur, Sun; 3pm-1am Fri; noon-1am Sat. **Meals served** *Yo! Sushi* noon-10pm daily. *Yo! Below* 5.30-10pm Mon-Thur, Sun; 3-11pm Fri; noon-11pm Sat. **Average** £. **Credit** AmEx, MC, V.

The London sushi bar chain finally landed in Scotland in 2001 and has been a big hit given the sheer lack of Japanese eateries north of the border, let alone in Edinburgh. It's the same formula as London: seats at the bar and booths, and a moving conveyor belt with plates carrying an astonishing variety of dishes prepared by chefs in the central kitchen space. You can stop for a minimalist bowl of miso soup or stuff yourself with plates and plates of prawn tempura, stir-fried vegetable noodles, assorted sashimi, maki and more. Yo! Sushi on the ground floor is the snack 'n' go part; Yo! Below downstairs is a more full-on restaurant experience with such extras as massage, tarot readings, music… Upstairs or down, this is not somewhere you go for a quiet night.

Fish & seafood

The Mussel Inn

61-65 Rose Street (225 5979/www.mussel-inn.com). Princes Street buses. **Meals served** noon-10pm Mon-Sat; 12.30-10pm Sun. **Average** ££. **Credit** AmEx, DC, MC, V.

Edinburgh's seafood canteen par excellence. Decor-wise, there are no frills. The signature dish is a kilo pot of mussels that comes in a variety of flavours from 'natural' (unadorned) to 'Spanish' (with tomato, green olives and chorizo). If mussels aren't your thing, you could start with seafood chowder or crab spring rolls, then move on to grilled platters of scallops in various sauces or king scallops stir-fried with egg noodles, ginger, garlic and pak choi. There are one or two veggie dishes and the odd alternative to shellfish, but not many. Lagers, including Corona and Budvar, are chalked up on a blackboard; desserts are as simple as apple crumble. But it's the mussels most people come for. Chips are extra, mind.

Mediterranean

Café Marlayne

76 Thistle Street (226 2230). Princes Street buses. **Meals served** noon-2pm, 6-10pm Tue-Sat. **Average** ££. **Credit** MC, V.

The Thistle Street area isn't short of places to eat, but Café Marlayne manages to stand out as an intelligent French option and has certainly built up a committed

The best restaurants

The Atrium
The restaurant that took Edinburgh dining to a new level in the early 1990s – still excellent. *See p125.*

(fitz)Henry
Quietly confident in Leith. *See p83.*

Number One
Grand hotel dining, established and assured. *See p62.*

Restaurant Martin Wishart
The most technically accomplished in the city. *See p85.*

The Tower
Above the Museum of Scotland; a cultured approach upstairs and down. *See p33.*

Vermilion
Up-and-coming restaurant in the new-wave Scotsman Hotel. *See p27.*

The Witchery/The Secret Garden
Edinburgh's destination diner for romantics and tourists. Top notch when it's on form. *See p34.*

coterie of fans. It can be a real relief to sneak in here for lunch to escape the bustle of Frederick and George Streets; wicker chairs and solid wooden tables help along the impression of a polite but relaxed environment. Starters include smoked haddock chowder and breast of pigeon with lentils; mains might be guinea fowl supreme with leeks and gruyère or roast sole with tartare sauce. Puds include a yummy sticky toffee pudding. The food can be accomplished and is certainly affordable, but the restaurant is not large, so it's wise to book.

Le Café St Honoré ★
35 Thistle Street Lane West (226 2211/www.icscotland. co.uk/cafe-sthonore). Bus 13, 23, 27, 42. **Meals served** noon-2.15pm, 7-10pm Mon-Fri; noon-2.15pm, 6-10pm Sat. **Average** £££. **Credit** AmEx, MC, DC, V.
Imagine if you will that Toulouse-Lautrec is still bristling with libido, and the cancan dancers in the corner are wrecked on absinthe. Mind you, being middle-class Le

Café St Honoré the dancers would be politely asked to leave. This restaurant recalls nothing more than fin-de-siècle Paris in decor, while the food is distinctly French with an occasional modern international twist. There might be grilled oysters with crayfish, bacon and gruyère to start, but also warm salad of scallops, chicken tikka and chorizo. Mains are a little more traditional: boeuf bourguignon with mash or lamb rump with creamed haricots, spinach and mint sauce. There's a great selection of house wines by the glass, and desserts are as you might expect (crème brûlée, tarte tatin, artisan cheeses).

Tapas Olé

10 Eyre Place (556 2754). Bus 23, 27, 36. **Meals served** noon-3pm, 6-10pm Mon-Thur; noon-10pm Fri, Sat; 1-10pm Sun. **Average** £. **Credit** MC, V.
Tapas Olé is big and bright, with a red and yellow decor (the colours of the Spanish flag) and windows that let the light flood in. It looks more in tune with large parties than intimate dining, although a table for two won't be a problem. At the last count there were around 40 different tapas to choose from, including the happily named pollo infierno ('hell's chicken': chicken in spices with tomato and chilli). A tapas-like tiger prawns in chilli and garlic comes to the table sizzling attractively, while the benchmark for a tapas establishment is surely tortilla espanola, and the version here is pretty good. If you can't be bothered picking and choosing, there's a set menu for £13 that offers a selection. Puddings (ice-cream or a pedestrian crème caramel) are strangely reminiscent of children's TV. Rumbustious and fun – but don't bother with dessert.
Branch: 4 Forrest Road, Old Town (225 7069).

Middle Eastern

Nargile

73 Hanover Street (225 5755/www.nargile.co.uk).
Princes Street buses. **Open** noon-2.30pm, 5.30-10pm Mon-Thur; noon-2.30pm, 5.30-11pm Fri, Sat. Closed 1wk Sept. **Average** ££. **Credit** AmEx, MC, V.
Welcome to the Turkish kitchen in the city centre. Nargile arrived in 2000, a sister restaurant to the original venture in Aberdeen. Decor-wise, it's bright, modern and cliché-free, while the extensive menu has meze as a big feature, but also kebabs, couscous, seafood, veggie options and specials – some Turkish wines too. The meze dinner is a good way to sample a wide range of tastes (from the expected houmous to midye piyaz – mussels with onion, white wine and herb sauce). Couscous choices include a traditional one (with lamb, carrots and potatoes), while the specials offer the likes

The **California Coffee Co** has put baristas and equipment into old police boxes around the city. There's one outlet towards the east end of Rose Street, not far from the Sainsbury's on the corner of St Andrew Square.

of fener baligi izgara (char-grilled skewers of monkfish tail, served on a tomato and black olive sauce). Desserts can be anything from fudge cake to profiteroles to a selection of Turkish sweets. Kebab houses aside, Turkish cuisine is rare in Scotland, and Nargile has managed to jam a welcome foot in the door.

Modern European

Duck's at Le Marché Noir ★

2-4 Eyre Place (558 1608/www.ducks.co.uk). Bus 23, 27, 36. **Meals served** 7-10.30pm Mon, Sat, Sun; noon-2.30pm, 7-10.30pm Tue-Fri. **Average £££. Credit** AmEx, DC, MC, V.

Duck's offers an intimate and polite (but not overly so) setting on the fringe of Edinburgh's New Town, with a lot of stress put on both food and good service. The wine list is also quite a wonder to behold, with numerous affordable bottles as well as examples of top-end Bordeaux that don't even carry a price. The bargain lunch menu can involve a herb-rich tomato and rosemary soup starter and a crafted main such as cod on herb and mustard potato salad, complemented very nicely by a caper vinaigrette. Dessert? Passionfruit parfait with coconut ice-cream is just fabulous. The à la carte menu entails a range of tastes from crispy duck, mango and cashew salad with lime and coriander dressing (as a starter) to halibut with polenta crust on fennel and sun-blush tomato salad (as a main). The care that proprietor Malcolm Duck brings to bear has established his restaurant as a real player on the local scene.

Harvey Nichols Forth Floor

Harvey Nichols, 30-34 St Andrew Square (524 8350/ www.harveynichols.com). Princes Street buses. **Open** 10am-5pm Mon; 10am-11pm Tue-Sat; noon-5pm Sun. **Meals served** noon-5pm Mon, Sun; noon-11pm Tue-Sat. **Average £££. Credit** AmEx, DC, MC, V.

There are only two contenders for the title of 'best restaurant in an Edinburgh retail outlet' and this is one (the other is Zinc; *see p85*). The swish people's posh shop arrived in the Scottish capital in autumn 2002 with its usual expensive (Harvey) knick-knacks, but also a restaurant and bar-brasserie perched on top. Key question: would you want to eat there? Simple answer: yes. The overall impression is '1970s funky' moderated by modern panache – imagine a high-class *Space 1999* canteen – with a lot of glass and a balcony, hence cool views of Edinburgh Castle and the Firth of Forth (hence the punning name – it's also on the fourth floor). And the food? A typical three-course meal in the bar-brasserie would be prosciutto and rocket salad with

Harvey Nichols Forth Floor

celeriac and mustard remoulade, followed by an ample portion of tender lamb shank with creamy parmesan polenta, and then a deft panna cotta. There's a discreet, transparent division between the all-day buzz of the bar-brasserie (the shoppers' favourite) and the more formal and expensive restaurant, where evening meals would be the appropriate choice.

Hurricane Bar & Grill

45 North Castle Street (226 0770/www.hurricane restaurants.com). Bus 26, 44, 129, Princes Street buses. **Meals served** noon-2.30pm, 6-10.30pm Mon-Thur; noon-2.30pm, 6-10.45pm Fri, Sat. **Average ££. Credit** AmEx, MC, V.

Hurricane arrived on the scene in 2002 with a pedigree chef in the shape of Alan Mathieson (formerly at the Atrium; *see p125*), a ground-level restaurant with yellow walls, leather seating and chrome fittings, and a basement bar with a grown-up cocktail menu as well as snack food. Downstairs eating could involve sandwiches (ribeye steak), salads (char-grilled Thai beef) or just coffee and bitter chocolate tart. Upstairs is where it gets serious. A typical three-courser could be confit duck and foie gras terrine, followed by venison loin with herb crust, and cranberry crème brûlée for pud. You could have a grill as a main, of course; these come with thick-cut chips and a choice of sauces (peppercorn, hollandaise and so on) to go with meats like lamb chops and assorted steaks. If you

The **Pizza Express** branch in Stockbridge at 1 Deanhaugh Street (332 7229) is one of the few places in Edinburgh where you can dine next to a river – albeit the Water of Leith.

want to start the evening with a decent Whisky Sour downstairs, then pop up for a 10oz sirloin steak and chips, Hurricane's your place.

Martins ★

70 Rose Street North Lane, between Frederick Street & Castle Street (225 3106). Princes Street buses. **Meals served** noon-2pm, 7-10pm Tue-Fri; 7-10pm Sat. Closed last wk Dec, 3wks Jan. **Average** £££. **Credit** AmEx, DC, MC, V.

Not easy to find but worth the effort, Martin Irons' tasteful and welcoming backstreet restaurant is a showcase for Scottish produce; he realised the value of attentive sourcing and organic ingredients years before most. From the vegetables to the meat and the fish, Irons insists that, as far as possible, everything is just as nature intended. The reward for such persistence has been an enviable reputation in the city – and beyond – since opening in 1983. A typical three-course dinner would involve foie gras terrine, toasted brioche and red onion marmalade to start; seared loin of wild venison, potato and mushroom gratin, braised red cabbage, roasted root vegetables and thyme jus as a main; and dark chocolate fondant with sable biscuit, blood orange compote and espresso syrup to finish. The artisan cheeseboard is among the very finest in Edinburgh.

The best outdoor spots

Lothian Street
Both **Negociants** (*see p43*) and the **Iguana** (*see p42*) have tables outside in summer.

Broughton Street
There's a beer garden at the **Outhouse** (*see p90*), and outside tables at **PopRokit** (*see p95*) and **Baroque** (*see p87*).

Leith
The Shore (*see p79*) is best on the east side of the Water of Leith, the **Waterfront** (*see p85*) on the west side.

The Grassmarket
Lots of ordinary pubs, but lots of pavement tables for an alfresco pint.

Royal Mile/Hunter's Square
Particularly during August try **Café Hub** (*see p37*), **EH1** (*see p40*) or **Bann UK** (*see p28*).

Number One ★

The Balmoral Hotel, 1 Princes Street (557 6727/
www.thebalmoralhotel.com). Princes Street buses.
Meals served noon-2pm, 7-10pm Mon-Thur; noon-2pm,
7-10.30pm Fri; 7-10.30pm Sat; 7-10pm Sun. Closed 1wk
Jan. **Average** ££££. **Credit** AmEx, DC, MC, V.
The Balmoral is the Victorian railway hotel at the east
end of Princes Street. Number One is its flagship
restaurant. Downstairs, away from the bustle of the city's
main thoroughfare, you enter a placid and classy world
of deft service and even more dextrous cuisine: chef Jeff
Bland earned a Michelin star at the beginning of 2003,
currently one of only two in the city (Restaurant Martin
Wishart in Leith has the other; *see p85*). There are red
lacquer walls, scalloped banquettes and a wine list to
intimidate or delight depending on your level of self-
esteem on the day. The food can be very good indeed, and
the set lunch is actually excellent value for money. For
that you might have a venison salad with truffle dressing,
followed by pan-fried halibut then dark chocolate terrine
and crème fraîche. If you go à la carte, you're talking a
three-course extravaganza, including the likes of air-dried
barbary duck, wild sea bass (none of your farmed muck)
and parfait of prune d'Agen – for more than twice the
price. Be brave. Step over that threshold.

Oloroso ★

*33 Castle Street (226 7614/www.oloroso.co.uk). Princes
Street buses.* **Meals served** noon-2.30pm, 7-10.30pm
daily. **Average** £££. **Credit** AmEx, MC, V.
Oloroso was one of Edinburgh's biggest restaurant
openings of 2001, but its early period seemed to be
affected by the illness of co-founder James Sankey, who

Rick's. *See p68.*

Although Fishers in Leith (*see p77*) is the original restaurant, many diners prefer the buzz at **Fishers in the City** at 58 Thistle Lane (225 5109).

sadly died in late 2002. His partner Tony Singh carried on, and diners should be grateful. The ground-floor entrance may be baffling – only a flat-screen video hints at what lies above – but once out of the lift everything is clear. The establishment occupies the top (fourth) floor of an office building, which means excellent all-round views. There's a very smart bar where you can drink or snack (deft Alsatian tart, fine samosas), and a restaurant space for the full dining experience. A typical starter would be seared tuna with artichoke hearts; a main might be corn-fed chicken with sage and parmesan polenta; then, to finish, espresso tart with vanilla ice-cream. The grill menu offers top-grade, and top-price, Highland beef – an 8oz fillet steak will cost £26 a head, with a choice of sauces (chilli jam or salsa verde, for instance). Food and service are right up there. The self-opinion of the clientele can tend to be right up there too, unfortunately.

Scottish

Haldane's ★

39A Albany Street (556 8407/www.haldanesrestaurant. com). Bus 8, 13, 17. **Meals served** noon-1.30pm, 6-9.30pm Mon-Fri; 6-9.30pm Sat, Sun. **Average £££.** **Credit** AmEx, DC, MC, V.
If a good Scottish restaurant is one that is run by Scots, uses the best of local ingredients and serves dishes with a Scots slant (but no gimmickry), then Haldane's qualifies in spades. Indeed, some regard it as the best Scottish restaurant in the city. Housed in the basement of the Albany Townhouse Hotel on the eastern fringes of the New Town, it has been building a steady reputation and

clientele since it opened in 1997. The main dining room looks out on to the garden, and there's also a 'study' room for more intimate meals. The decor is discreet and tasteful. A full three courses could bring baked oak-smoked salmon and leek tart with white wine and mussel sauce to start; Scottish beef fillet topped with brandy and black peppercorn sabayon; then sticky toffee pudding with vanilla ice-cream for dessert. The wine list is good and there are lots of single malts. Very fine indeed.

Henderson's Salad Table & Wine Bar

94 Hanover Street (225 2131/www.hendersonsof edinburgh.co.uk). Bus 11, 13, 23, 27. **Meals served** 8am-10.30pm Mon-Sat; noon-9pm Sun. **Average** £. **Credit** AmEx, DC, MC, V.

Unbelievable as it may seem, this establishment dates back to 1963 when the idea of a vegetarian canteen in Edinburgh was probably as amusing as the Beatles being a major cultural force. In the 1960s and '70s it really was way out on its own; not so much now. Basically, it's a self-service restaurant, with seating on the counter level where people can eat and go, or you can wander down a few stairs to linger in the cellar space (sometimes with live music). There are good organic wines and beers,

Henderson's shop is upstairs from the famous vegetarian canteen and sells all kinds of meat-free snack food.

Snack attack

Edinburgh has its share of small cafés, fast-food bars and takeaways: places you can buy a snack or a drink to have on the hop, or spend a few minutes guzzling indoors. The global giants are here, of course: **McDonald's** and **Burger King** both have prominent branches on Princes Street (at opposite ends), while the recent expansion of **Starbucks** leaves those of an entrepreneurial bent breathless (three at the beginning of 2000, 13 now).

Then there's the Irish sandwich bar **O'Briens** (eight branches), coffee chain **Costa** (seven) and the rather more upmarket sandwich bar **Pret A Manger** (three). Meanwhile, since 1996 the **California Coffee Company** has operated out of old police boxes dotted around the city, selling what many regard as the best takeaway coffee in Edinburgh.

In among all the exalted 'brands', however, there is one name that seldom gets mentioned: humble old **Greggs the Baker**. Greggs is hardly a Scottish phenomenon; its roots lie in the north-east of England. But from a standing start 40 years ago (one shop), Greggs now has more than 1,100 branches across the UK, including an incredible 22

substantial salads that constitute meals in themselves (celery, apple and hazelnut; cabbage with apple and raisin) and trenchant main courses: mushroom savoury with tomato and basil, or vegetarian haggis, mashed turnip (swede – you're in Scotland) and potato. Desserts – fruit salad or dried fruit with sour cream and ginger – are as healthy and wholesome as everything else.

Keepers

13B Dundas Street (556 5707). Bus 23, 27. **Meals served** noon-2pm, 6-10pm Tue-Fri; 6-10pm Sat. Closed 1wk Jan, 1wk Apr, 1wk July, 1wk Oct. **Average £££. Credit** AmEx, MC, V.

A Scottish restaurant that has lasted the course, Keepers is a basement space with cosy dining areas, bare stone walls and a warm, traditional feel. Game and other Scottish ingredients feature large, carefully confected into rich comforting dishes. Try the likes of oysters or duck liver (starters), saddle of hare or Aberdeen Angus beef (mains) and Drambuie crème brûlée (dessert). There's always one veggie choice on the menu. Positioned on one of the main thoroughfares through the Georgian New Town, Keepers offers one particular strand of the Caledonian experience. You suspect Sir Walter Scott might eat here if he were still alive, but he died in 1832.

in the Scottish capital – more even than Starbucks or McDonald's.

It sells cheap sandwiches, cakes, soft drinks and freshly baked pies and pasties. The formula is to mass produce the savouries at a central plant, then ship them out to the shops to be baked on the premises – so most Greggs smell nicely of chicken or cheese pasties, or sausage rolls, that have just emerged from the oven.

The crucial issue? Price. Where a coffee and a sandwich at Starbucks can sometimes leave you little change from a £5 note, a Greggs pastie will give you change from a £1 coin. The queues outside every Greggs at lunchtime are testament to their popularity. Although the outfit doesn't have the kiddie appeal of McDonald's, coffee like the California Coffee Company or aspirational snacks like Pret, it offers astonishing value – which is important to know if you're on a budget and want to fill up.

In the New Town, there's a handy branch at **85-87 Rose Street** (226 1952). One warning: catch the savouries when they're hot and fresh. A cold cheese pastie isn't a gastronomic delight.

Café-bars & Cafés

Au Gourmand

1 Brandon Terrace (624 4666). Bus 8, 17. **Open** 8am-5.30pm Mon-Sat; 10am-5pm Sun. **Credit** MC, V.

New on the scene in 2002, Au Gourmand is essentially a very accomplished pâtisserie/boulangerie with a café-bar space at the rear. It's been stripped back to bare stone so offers a fairly minimal environment, but with some of the best French snacking in the city. Alcohol is limited to wine (and you have to ask for the list), but there are assorted crêpes, assiettes of charcuterie and fromage and excellent ample sandwiches (the 'simple' comprises farmhouse pâté, salad and gherkin on good French bread). Service comes from polite young women. The more mature New Town lady would linger here over a coffee and newspaper of a morning.

Glass & Thompson ★

2 Dundas Street (557 0909). Bus 23, 27. **Open** 8.30am-5.30pm Mon-Sat; 11am-4.30pm Sun. **Credit** AmEx, MC, V.

A cross between a deli and a café, Glass & Thompson sits on one of New Town's main thoroughfares. It has a modern look, a few tables (with a couple outside in summer) and offers some great snacks. That means tarts (asparagus and fennel; ricotta and pine nut) or one of the establishment's signature platters, such as Colston Basset stilton with pear, salad and bread, brie de Meaux with fresh fruit and salad, or smoked salmon. There's also assorted antipasti, dolmádes and falafel, and a very small selection of wine and bottled beer. The cakes are amazing too, with the likes of tarte au citron and orange and almond syrup cake. It's in the New Town, however, so class warriors will find the accents of some staff as attractive as nails scraped down a blackboard.

Opal Lounge

51A George Street (226 2275/www.opallounge.co.uk). Princes Street buses. **Open** noon-3am daily. **Meals served** noon-10pm daily. **Average** £. **Credit** AmEx, MC, V.

The Opal Lounge hit the city centre with a design flourish in 2002 and instantly became the place to see and be seen. Housed in a basement, the interior looks contemporary, cool and minimal: a kind of dark chic. As a bar, it's big on cocktails (complicated champagne 'mixes', for instance) and even offers entire bottles of spirits (Skyy vodka, £70). Most customers opt for the more economical bottled lager or sub-£20 wines. On the food front, it's predominantly oriental: 'bites' (prawn wun tuns, seared tuna sashimi), soups (chicken dumpling and noodle),

Café Royal.
See p70.

more substantial 'bowls' (blackened pork and egg-fried noodles) and bento boxes in chicken, beef or prawn flavours. And is that Prince William over there?

Rick's

55A Frederick Street (622 7800/www.ricksedinburgh.co.uk). Princes Street buses. **Open** 7am-1am daily. **Meals served** 7am-11pm daily. **Average** ££. **Credit** AmEx, MC, V.

More than just somewhere to drink, Rick's is also a restaurant and a small boutique hotel. The venue attracts central Edinburgh trendies and occasional top-flight footballers (from Scotland and England) with mandatory blondes on their arm. On busy nights, this is certainly not a venue for a quiet romantic dinner, but the food is well done. The choice is wide: you can throw back a couple of pints of Guinness with a dozen oysters or go through an international three-course experience. To start, try smoked duck with mixed leaves and sour cherry chutney, or monkfish and prosciutto skewer with saffron sauce. There are assorted main courses, grills, vegetarian choices and salads. A simple grill (tuna on coriander mash, with chilli oil and crisped red onions) is substantial and neatly prepared, while a main such as coconut basil chicken with steamed rice also hits the spot. Desserts are adequate, but many people come for the booze – good tequila, decent cocktails – and the buzz.

The Watershed

44 St Stephen Street (220 3774). Bus 34, 36. **Open** 11am-midnight Mon-Thur, Sun; 11am-1am Fri, Sat. **Meals served** 11am-8pm Mon-Fri; 11am-6pm Sat, Sun. **Average** £. **Credit** MC, V.

Raeburn Place, Stockbridge, is blessed with not one but two good delicatessens: **Peckham's** at No.48 (332 8844) and **Herbie's** at No.66 (332 9888).

A personable style bar in the quintessential Stockbridge street, the Watershed is a basement establishment with a distressed wooden floor, quiet colours and designer seating. Its drinks menu offers some decent bottled lager (Peroni, Budvar), as well as eight affordable wines and a reasonable cocktail list. Food-wise, during the week there are starters and snacks (Thai fish cakes, nachos), open sandwiches (minute steak) and burgers (including vegetarian), and a creative brunch menu at weekends. This includes choices like eggs florentine or toasted courgette bread with spinach, sun-dried tomatoes and goat's cheese. On quiet weekday afternoons, you can eavesdrop while young New Town ladies discuss menfolk called Jamie or Euan and their Foreign Office careers. Later, it's the usual posse of people knocking back happy-hour jugs of Mai Tai.

Whighams Wine Cellars

*13 Hope Street, Charlotte Square (225 9717/
www.whighams.co.uk). Princes Street buses.* **Open** noon-
11pm Mon; noon-midnight Tue-Thur; noon-1am Fri, Sat.
Meals served noon-10pm Mon-Thur; noon-9pm Fri, Sat.
Average ££. Credit AmEx, MC, V.
Just off the west end of Princes Street, this is a well-
established basement wine bar with a real 'cellar' feel.
The small alcoves off the main bar space have low
ceilings (not for the claustrophobic), but they are
atmospheric, especially in candlelight, while the decor is
minimal to the point of non-existence. The wine choice is
good (around 100 bins, with 30 or so available by the
glass) and the competent menu has a seafood slant. That
means starters such as smoked salmon or mussels with

garlic and parsley butter, and mains like Arbroath smokies or crab cakes with chilli mayonnaise. Tiramisu is a simple but typical dessert, although the cheese board has many fans. Popular with the financial services crowd from nearby offices, but a good hideaway for anyone.

Pubs & Bars

Café Royal Circle Bar/Oyster Bar ★

Circle Bar: 19 West Register Street (556 1884). Oyster Bar: 17A West Register Street (556 4124). Princes Street buses. **Open** *Circle Bar* 11am-11pm Mon-Wed; 11am-midnight Thur; 11am-1am Fri, Sat; 12.30-11pm Sun. **Meals served** *Circle Bar* 11am-10pm Mon-Sat; 12.30-10pm Sun. *Oyster Bar* noon-2pm, 7-10pm daily. **Average** *Circle Bar* £. *Oyster Bar* £££. **Credit** AmEx, DC, MC, V.
A wonderful old island bar dominates this classic bar where the walls are decorated with Royal Doulton tiled pictures of famous inventors (Caxton, Faraday, Watt and the like) – a Victorian paean to progress. You'll usually find several cask ales on offer, up to 20 single malts, even some wine, and if you can't cram yourself into the leather booths there's lots of standing room. Tourists love its authenticity, locals love the fact that the Café Royal just seems to last forever. The adjacent Café Royal Oyster Bar beyond the partition is, if anything, an even grander affair. A destination restaurant before the term was

Guildford Arms. *See p72.*

Bert's (*see p132*) other bar at 2-4 Raeburn Place (332 6345) offers faux tradition and a good pint in the heart of Stockbridge.

coined, it prides itself on rich, old-school fish dishes, which it does remarkably well. Three courses might involve half a dozen oysters on ice to start, fillet of salmon in camembert and white wine sauce with poached mussels and prawns as a main, and then one of the restaurant's simply awesome brûlées (rowanberry and elderflower, perhaps) for dessert.

Clark's Bar

142 Dundas Street (556 1067). Bus 27, 33. **Open** 11am-11pm Mon-Wed, Sun; 11am-11.30pm Thur-Sat. **No credit cards**.

Sparse and traditional, this old, Victorian-looking 'howf' has red leather seats, polished red linoleum on the floor, shiny brass table tops and a dark red ceiling. It hasn't changed in years, and the effect is a bit like walking into a pound of liver. The best beers on tap are the locally brewed Caledonian 80/- and its sister pint, Deuchars IPA. The whisky selection is reasonable, the food basic (toasties and baguettes) and there's often football on the TV. The proximity of big financial services offices means there are occasional men in suits, but Clark's is a welcome find given the sore lack of pubs in the New Town.

The Cumberland ★

1-3 Cumberland Street (558 3134). Bus 23, 27. **Open** 11am-1am daily. **Credit** MC, V.

One of Edinburgh's classic cask ale pubs, the Cumberland is a very well-kept establishment bang in the heart of the New Town. Its decor is predominantly wooden, with a nod to tradition, but light and spacious. It's no misogynist drinking den, however; there's a selection of wine and a rustic beer garden (sheer joy in summer if you can get a seat). The nine or so cask ales on tap change regularly, but you'll find the likes of Dark Island or Red MacGregor from Orkney, as well as English guests such as Timothy Taylor's Landlord or Hop Back's Summer Lightning. Bar food includes toasties and paninis. A damned fine hostelry.

FOPP

7-15 Rose Street (220 0310/www.fopp.co.uk). Princes Street buses. **Open** noon-9pm Mon-Sat; 1-6pm Sun. **Credit** AmEx, MC, V.

FOPP is the kind of music shop (cheap CDs, vinyl, cut-price pop culture books and DVDs) that you learn to love very quickly. It has shops in 11 UK cities and in 2002 it opened its second in Edinburgh (the original is at 55 Cockburn Street in the Old Town). But the tidy new Rose Street branch brought something extra: a bar. It's in a corner of the first floor, seats six (or eight close mates), with standing room for a few more, and sells bottled beer and wine only: £10 per bottle of wine and £2 per beer, such as Hoegaarden, Pilsner Urquell and Beck's. So if you're dithering over which CD to buy, stop and have a drink instead. Genius.

Guildford Arms ★

1-5 West Register Street (556 4312). Princes Street buses.
Open 11am-11pm Mon-Thur; 11am-midnight Fri, Sat;
12.30-11pm Sun. **Credit** AmEx, MC, V.
A Victorian drinking palace with a few nooks and crannies, and a very high ceiling, the Guildford is bang in the city centre, but quite discreet given its position a few yards off the east end of Princes Street. It has an excellent, rotating selection of cask ales with a few rarities (Schiehallion cask-conditioned lager from the Harviestoun Brewery, for instance) and caters to a very mixed crowd: office workers, rugby fans on international matchdays, students, harassed shoppers looking for a haven. It's ornate, it does pub food, but the beer's the thing.

Kay's ★

39 Jamaica Street West (225 1858). Bus 13, 28.
Open 11am-midnight Mon-Thur; 11am-1am Fri, Sat;
12.30-11pm Sun. **Credit** MC, V.
This building housed a wine merchant's for more than 150 years until it morphed into a pub in 1976 – so drink has been the mainstay here for the best part of two centuries. It now has a reputation as a somewhat patrician New Town 'howf' with a good selection of draught beer (Timothy Taylor's Landlord, Brakspear from Henley on Thames, Scottish examples) and an excellent choice of around 50 single malt whiskies, some of them fairly rare and fairly pricey. The decor is predominantly red and old-fashioned. A great place to sit one wet afternoon and work your way along that whisky shelf.

The Oxford Bar

8 Young Street (539 7119/www.oxfordbar.com). Princes Street buses. **Open** 11am-1am Mon-Sat; 12.30-1am Sun.
No credit cards.
The Oxford has one of the most cramped bar spaces in the city; the walls in the side room are the colour of congealed English mustard; and there's a general air of dowdiness that complements the establishment's odd bare lightbulb. So why drink here? Because despite the fact that temples of swank such as Oloroso (*see p62*) and Hurricane (*see p59*) are only a few minutes' walk away, this backstreet bar cussedly ploughs its own furrow and gives not a damn for the white noise of contemporary style. You can get Deuchars IPA, you can get a good whisky and you can actually stand (or sit) and talk with your mates without cheesy house blaring in the background. The Oxford also has minor celebrity status as a haunt of Inspector Rebus from the Ian Rankin novels.

Edinburgh:
North-east
& Leith

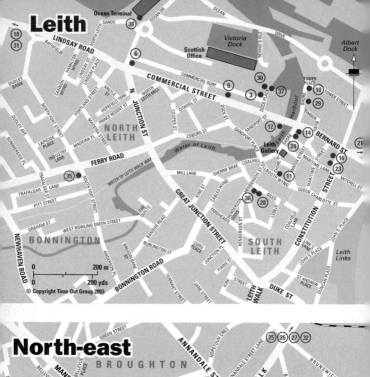

Leith

- 18
- 31

LINDSAY ROAD

Ocean Terminal 38

OCEAN DR

OCEAN

SANDS

NORTH LEITH MILL

Victoria Dock

RENNIE'S ISLE

DRIVE

Albert Dock

BATHFIELD

DUDLEY BANK

CANNON WYND

HAMILTON WYND

LINDSAY ST

LINDSAY PLACE

ARGYLE ST

Scottish Office

COMMERCIAL QUAY

6

PORTLAND STREET

HOPEFIELD TERR

HOPEFIELD REGENT ST

N JUNCTION ST

COMMERCIAL STREET

9

30

3

37

TOWER PLACE

10 TOWER STREET

29

NORTH FORT STREET

NORTH LEITH ST

MADEIRA TERR

MADEIRA PL

NORTH LEITH

CITADEL ST

COUPER ST

DOCK ST

SANDPORT ST

DOCK ST

SHORE

Harbour

TIMBER

DUDLEY AVE

NORTH JUNCTION STREET

LAPICIDE PLACE

INDUSTRY LANE

FERRY ROAD

COBURG ST

12

14

BERNARD ST

21

SUMMERSIDE PL

MADEIRA ST

Water of Leith

Leith Gallery

SHORE

24

16

23

TRAFALGAR ST

SOUTH FORT STREET

Water of Leith Walk Way

MILL LANE

SHERRIFF BRAE

KING ST

CABLES WYND

COALHILL

HENDERSON ST

GILES

STREET

TOLBOOTH WYND

11

WATER STREET

MARITIME LANE

QUEEN CHARLOTTE ST

MITCHELL ST

35

PITT STREET

GRAHAM ST

WEST BOWLING GREEN STREET

YARDHEADS

36

28

FERGUSON

HENDERSON

COALFIELD

CONSTITUTION

INN'S LANE

BONNINGTON

NEWHAVEN ROAD

BANGOR ROAD

BROAD LANE

ANDERSON PL

BURLINGTON ST

CORU PLACE

JUNCTION PL

GREAT JUNCTION STREET

PIRRIE ST

JANE STREET

SOUTH LEITH

ST ANDREW PLACE

DUNCAN PLACE

JOHN'S LANE

JOHN'S PLACE

Leith Links

0   200 m
0   200 yds

© Copyright Time Out Group 2003

BONNINGTON ROAD

TENNANT STREET

KIRK STREET

LEITH WALK

DUKE ST

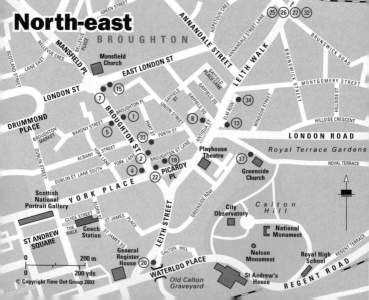

North-east

GREEN STREET

BROUGHTON

MANSFIELD PL

BELLEVUE PLACE

ANNANDALE STREET

25 26 27 32

HOPETOUN CRES

BRUNSWICK ROAD

SCOTLAND STREET

BELLEVUE CRES

LANE EAST

Mansfield Church

EAST LONDON ST

ANNANDALE STREET LANE

LEITH WALK

MONTGOMERY STREET

LONDON ST

7 15

GAYFIELD PLACE LANE

GAYFIELD ST

GAYFIELD SQ

BRUNSWICK STREET

HILLSIDE ST

DRUMMOND PLACE

BROUGHTON PL

BROUGHTON ST

1

BARONY STREET

UNION STREET

8

34

ELM ROW

WINDSOR STREET

HILLSIDE CRESCENT

BROUGHTON MARKET

5

33

HART ST

FORTH ST

13

LONDON ROAD

DUBLIN STREET

YORK LANE

ALBANY STREET

2

YORK LANE

BROUGHTON ST LANE

Royal Terrace Gardens

DUBLIN ST LANE SOUTH

4

19

Playhouse Theatre

17

ROYAL TERRACE

22

PICARDY PL

Greenside Church

Scottish National Portrait Gallery

YORK PLACE

LEITH STREET

GREENSIDE ROW

Calton Hill

City Observatory

CLYDE STREET

ELDER STREET

National Monument

REGENT TERRACE

ST ANDREW SQUARE

THE WALK

ST JAMES PLACE

Coach Station

ST JAMES SQ

CALTON HILL

Nelson Monument

Royal High School

General Register House

20

WATERLOO PLACE

St Andrew's House

Old Calton Graveyard

REGENT ROAD

0   200 m
0   200 yds

© Copyright Time Out Group 2003

Leith has served as Edinburgh's port for centuries, even though Leithers have always had a fair sense of their own identity; in 1833 it was even granted burgh status. But urban development in the 19th century brought Edinburgh and Leith closer together, and in 1920 the City of Edinburgh formally scooped up its neighbour, despite protests. This explains a lot. The area immediately north-east of Princes Street (including Broughton Street) still feels relatively central, but the main hub of eating and drinking in Leith itself, around the Shore, could be in another town altogether. Between the two, down Leith Walk and Easter Road, there are only a handful of establishments worth looking at.

Restaurants

Asian

Britannia Spice

150 Commercial Street, Britannia Way (555 2255/ www.britanniaspice.co.uk). Bus 1, 16, 22, 35, 36, 49. **Meals served** noon-2.15pm, 5-11.45pm daily. **Average** ££. **Credit** AmEx, DC, MC, V.

(fitz)henry. *See p83.*

Not too far from the Royal Yacht *Britannia* (moored in Edinburgh as a tourist attraction), this nautical-themed restaurant tries to cover the whole subcontinent rather than just India, with some Thai thrown in for good measure. It gets a fair bit of business from the adjacent Holiday Inn, and generally draws the crowds. The menu includes all the usual suspects of Indian cooking, but much more besides. Maccher bhorta is a Bangladeshi baked fish starter with mustard oil, onions, chillies and coriander. Mains are as diverse as Himalayan momo (spicy mince dumplings), Mughlai vegetables (vegetables stuffed with coriander, almonds, cardamom and corn), padgra prao (seafood stir-fried with chilli and basil, Thai style) and macch torkari (Bangladeshi fish curry). The wine list is better than at many of its peers.

China China

10 Antigua Street (556 9791). Playhouse buses. **Open** noon-midnight daily. **Average** £. **Credit** AmEx, DC, MC, V.

Imagine a dirt-cheap Chinese canteen with a nod to IKEA design values and you've got China China. Basically, it costs a fiver at lunchtime, £8 early evening and a tenner at dinner – for an all-you-can-eat buffet. Drinks are extra; choices include a few wines and beers such as Tsingtao and Tiger. The food is pretty much canteen standard: Cantonese spare ribs, chicken wings, black bean beef, a

Indian restaurant **Suruchi Too** in Leith (121 Constitution Street, 554 3268) is sister to the original Suruchi in South Edinburgh (*see p105*).

couple of soups and chicken curry. You can end the meal with fresh fruit – top marks. It's all very jolly, obviously a real bargain, popular with families and often packed.

Fish & seafood

Fishers ★

1 The Shore (554 5666/www.fishersbistro.co.uk). Bus 1, 16, 22, 35, 36, 49. **Meals served** noon-4pm, 6-10.30pm Mon-Sat; 12.30-10.30pm Sun. **Average** ££. **Credit** AmEx, DC, MC, V.

The nautical decor at Fishers is pretty well justified by the fact that the harbour's on the doorstep and you can see real working ships as you walk down the Shore to the restaurant. Diners can eat in the bar or in the small raised area adjacent. It's essentially a fish restaurant, although there are a few meat choices; vegetarians should phone ahead. Starters include char-grilled marlin with a spiced crust and mango sauce, cold crevettes with aïoli, and a very moist and creamy crab, mascarpone and asparagus tart. The international influences are even more apparent in mains such as whole steamed sea bass with wilted greens and soy, and halibut fillet with apricot and curry sauce and lemongrass rice. Those opting for the simple (and legendary) fish cakes get a rich and robust portion. **Branch**: **Fishers in the City** 58 Thistle Lane, New Town (225 5109).

ANTIPASTA, PIZZA, PASTA, DOLCE, VINO, BIRRA, CAFFÉ

Vittoria

italian restaurant & caffé bar

113 brunswick st., leith walk.

t: 0131 556 6171   f: 0131 478 7009

e: info@vittoriarestaurant.com

www.vittoriarestaurant.com

Large smoking/non-smoking rooms
Alfresco dining

Open 7 days 10am - 11pm

12pm - 11pm Sundays

The Shore

3-4 The Shore (553 5080). Bus 1, 16, 22, 35, 36, 49.
Meals served noon-2.30pm; 6.30-10pm Mon-Fri; 12.30-3pm, 6.30-10pm Sat, Sun. **Average £££. Credit** AmEx, DC, MC, V.

The Shore qualifies as a 'proper restaurant' since its smart little dining space seems the main fixture here while the bar serves as an ante-room – although people do come for just a drink (Caledonian 80/-, Deuchars IPA and a nice selection of wines). In summer there are even seats outside; the more adventurous walk across the street and sit on the edge of the dock. The bar theme is nautical with wooden panelling, while the restaurant space is defined more by sparkling cutlery and white tablecloths. There's a seafood slant offering the likes of steamed mussels with garlic, shallots, white wine and cream to start, and sautéed monkfish and king scallops with saffron and garlic as a main. Yummy puds include chocolate mousse. Not destination dining, but a quality little establishment whether you eat or just stop for a pint.

Skippers

1A Dock Place (554 1018/www.skippers.co.uk). Bus 1, 16, 22, 35, 36, 49. **Meals served** noon-2pm, 7-10pm Mon-Fri; noon-2pm, 6.30-10.2pm Sat; 12.30-2.30pm, 7-10pm Sun. **Average ££. Credit** AmEx, MC, V.

Skippers has been around for more than 20 years and was a real pioneer in the pre-refurbished docklands of Leith. Through the 1980s and '90s it built a reputation as Edinburgh's best seafood bistro; current proprietors (Gavin and Karen Ferguson) have been in charge since 1999. The decor is attractively cluttered with a nod to the sea, and dishes range from the simple to complex. You could start with six large Loch Etive oysters, or a terrine of serrano ham, wild salmon and potato with chilli jam. Mains-wise, it's hard to beat the flavours in roasted Shetland langoustines with garlic and parsley butter, though marinated fillet of tuna with lime and coriander mayonnaise tries hard. There are some non-fish options, and the desserts are competent, though they don't really match courses one and two. But who cares? This is fishy heaven; watch for specials just pulled from the ocean.

Mediterranean

Daniel's

88 Commercial Street (553 5933). Bus 1, 16, 22, 35, 36, 49. **Meals served** 10am-10pm daily. **Average £. Credit** AmEx, MC, V.

A medal for the man from Alsace. The row of premises opposite Leith's large and intimidating Scottish Executive building has been a graveyard for restaurants

The best sit-in fish and chips in the city? **Ye Old Peacock Inn** (100 Lindsay Road, Newhaven, 552 8707). Popular with kids, it's around half a mile west of the Shore in the heart of Leith.

and bars – good and bad – ever since it was constructed in the 1990s. Daniel Vencker's place, however, was among the first and has lasted the course. It functions as a café-bar (coffee and croissant during the day if you want) as well as a full-on restaurant. The decor involves glass, light and blonde wood (sit in the conservatory if you can), while the fairly extensive menu has an Alsatian slant. There are starters, pizzas, tartes flambées, vegetarian specials, charcoal grills (double lamb chops in red wine jus, for example), traditional casserole dishes (beef bourguignon, cassoulet) and more. And you won't find a special like jarret de porc à l'alsacienne anywhere else in Edinburgh – a knuckle of pork on the bone, slowly cooked. Spicy ice-cream terrine or pain perdu, a French version of bread and butter pudding, are typical, and delicious, desserts.

Giuliano's on the Shore

1 Commercial Street (554 5272/www.giulianos.co.uk).
Bus 1, 16, 22, 35, 36, 49. **Meals served** noon-10.30pm daily. **Average** £. **Credit** AmEx, MC, V.
Kiddie heaven. Giuliano's is a bright, breezy Italian restaurant where the waiters seem specially trained to charm children. The decor is on the kitsch side, and the food won't garner a Michelin star, but the little ones wolf it up. There are around 25 starters – everything from avocado prawns to fried squid – then loads of pasta and pizza, steaks, chicken, veal and a special seafood menu depending on the catch of the day. To be honest, a kitchen geared up for pizza margharita by the dozen might not

See p89.

The **Sicilian Pastry Shop** (14-16 Albert Street, off Leith Walk, 554 7417) does great cakes and takeway Italian savouries.

be quite as adept at handling fresh scallops – but the kids still get their garlic bread with melted cheese, fizzy drinks and torta fantastica (layered vanilla/toffee ice-cream on a chocolate-coated biscuit base), while mum and dad have the same, plus penne, and can knock back the chianti. The branch near the Playhouse Theatre, near the top of Leith Walk, is not nearly as much fun.
Branch: Giuliano's No.1 18-19 Union Place, Leith Walk, North-east & Leith (556 6590).

The Jolly Pizzeria

9 Elm Row, Leith Walk (556 1588). Bus 7, 10, 12, 14, 16 22, 25, 49. **Meals served** 11.45am-2.15pm, 5-11pm daily. **Average £. Credit** AmEx, DC, MC, V.

Only snobs and imbeciles could fail to love this pizzeria. Establishments such as these are so often written off as throwbacks, but they're a more enduring part of Scottish working-class history (Italian influences on affordable eating out in the latter half of the 20th century) than any number of maudlin industrial museums. At the Jolly, the spectacularly bald maître d' has a hallucinogenic waistcoat; the decor was originally ethnic in the 1970s, but the world moved on and it evolved into kitsch by dint of doing nothing – and can you spot the Serie A club crests? Foodwise, the pizza toppings may not be sophisticated (sweetcorn and chilli, for instance), but the wood-burning oven creates the best pizza base in the city. There are also various standard pasta dishes, Italian lager and more. The desserts appeal to kids. In its own way, one of the most dignified restaurants in Edinburgh.

Ristorante Tinelli

139 Easter Road (652 1932). Bus 1, 35. **Meals served**
6-11pm Tue-Sat. **Average** ££. **Credit** AmEx, DC, MC, V.
Chef-owner Giancarlo Tinelli has been plying his trade
on unfashionable Easter Road since the early 1980s, and
his restaurant has changed little since then. When other
Italians were offering only pizza or penne piccante, Mr T
had much more interesting things on the menu – and he
still does. The long-serving waiters in the tiny dining
room are on good terms with their regulars who come
from far and wide. Air-dried beef with parmesan may no
longer be revolutionary, but it's still a fine starter. Fish
fans and vegetarians will have no anxieties, but Tinelli's
meat dishes are central: grilled liver, baked rabbit, steak
tartare, or escalope of veal rolled in mortadella and
spinach, in a red wine and clove sauce. The wine list is
short and functional, while desserts seem to be aimed at
children more than grown-ups.

The Tapas Tree

*1 Forth Street (556 7118/www.tapastree.co.uk). Bus 8,
17, Playhouse buses.* **Meals served** 11am-11pm daily.
Average £. **Credit** AmEx, DC, MC, V.
Get your Spanish head on, fingers in the patatas aïoli and
glug that rioja. The Tapas Tree is a down-home tapas
bar – tables crowd together upstairs, but it's a little more
spacious downstairs (where they occasionally have live
music and flamenco). There are daily specials on the
blackboard and a goodly range of substantial tapas
regulars: meat, vegetarian, fish/shellfish and skewered
things. There's serrano ham, Spanish salami, manchego
cheese, classic tortilla or marinated anchovies – but also
slightly more unusual options such as haunch of red deer
marinated in red wine, on a skewer. The house bread is
among the most substantial in Edinburgh, there are some
Spanish lagers and the wine list has a few bottles that are
better than you might imagine. A fun place.

The Vintners Rooms

*The Vaults, 87 Giles Street (554 6767). Bus 1, 7, 10, 14,
22.* **Meals served** noon-2pm, 7-10pm Mon-Sat. Closed
2wks Jan. **Average** £££. **Credit** AmEx, MC, V.
Housed in a highly atmospheric, 17th-century Leith wine
warehouse, the Vintners has tables by the bar (high
ceiling, lots of space) and another room adjacent (more
intimate, low-ceilinged, good for candlelight trysts). Very
traditional looking, it's a world away from the down-at-
heel housing in the vicinity. The daily changing menu
has a French slant, with such starters as tartelette aux
crabes or char-grilled scallops with saffron and mussel
sauce. The mains might be baked halibut with lobster
sherry broth, or braised partridge with puy lentils.

The **Deep Sea**
(2 Antigua
Street, Leith
Walk, 557
0276) is one
of Edinburgh's
finest fish and
chip shops.

There's no holding back with flavour, and if the cooking ever falls down on finesse, it usually makes up for it in the sheer bravado of taste. Almond, armagnac and prune tart is the kind of dessert you just don't want to miss; there's a good wine list too. The Vintners is the kind of restaurant that makes it worthwhile travelling to Leith.

Mexican

Salsa Hut

3A Albert Street (554 4344/www.oneclickdesign.co.uk/salsahut). Bus 7, 10, 12, 14, 16, 22, 25. **Meals served** 7-10.30pm daily. **Average £. No credit cards.**

Albert Street is far from salubrious. Opposite its west end lies the city's social work headquarters, while not far from the east end is the stadium of Hibernian FC. Middle class, it's not. But in among all this urban vérité lies the Salsa Hut, a mad neighbourhood cantina with an authentic hand-knitted feel. Seemingly run by slightly spacey young women who all have DJ boyfriends, it offers all the Mexican staples like enchiladas and burritos, adequately handled, and is actually quite a pleasant change for this neck of the woods (most of the local competition is dodgy kebab houses). Imagine a summer music festival dance tent meets tortilla chips 'n' dips on one of Leith's scabbier rows of tenements with a 'let's do the show right here' chutzpah. You can even bring in your own booze, hurrah.

Modern European

(fitz)Henry ★

19 Shore Place (555 6625/www.fitzhenrys.com). Bus 1, 16, 22, 35, 36, 49. **Meals served** 6.30-10pm Tue, Sat, Sun; noon-2.30pm, 6.30-10pm Wed-Fri. Closed 2wks Jan. **Average £££. Credit** AmEx, DC, MC, V.

The first time you step into (fitz)Henry, located on a quiet Leith backstreet, the change from outside to in is quite a contrast; the interior of the former 19th-century warehouse seems lush and minimal simultaneously. Conceived and delivered by Dave Ramsden, who now runs Rogue (*see p126*), this excellent restaurant was adopted in 2001 by two other experienced Edinburgh foodies: Alan Morrison and Val Faichney. The quality of cuisine has certainly been maintained; chef Hubert Lamort runs a skilled and adventurous kitchen. There's a modern French feel to the cooking: pan-fried ox tongue with oven-dried tomato and asparagus salad would be a typical starter, followed by braised lamb shank, polenta and parmesan mash and basil jus; finish with pine kernel tart and honey ice-cream. (Vegetarian diners should phone ahead and have a word, but it won't be a problem.)

(fiTZ) HENRY

FOOD : WINE : SERVICE : AMBIANCE

19 SHORE PLACE, LEITH, EDINBURGH

Restaurant Martin Wishart ★

54 The Shore (553 3557). Bus 1, 16, 22, 35, 36, 49.
Meals served noon-2pm, 7-9.30pm Tue Fri; 7-9.30pm
Sat. **Average** ££££. **Credit** AmEx, MC, V.
As one of only two establishments in the city with a
Michelin star, how good is this restaurant really? In foodie
terms, really very good. Wishart has worked under some
terribly famous names (a brace of Roux, Marco Pierre
White), and since opening in 1999 his diner has gained a
stratospheric reputation. Restaurant Martin Wishart isn't
huge (in a London Conran sense), but this means quality
control is impeccable. The service is confident enough to
be relaxed (but they'd probably frown at feet on the table)
and although it's generally formal it's not uptight. The
menu changes all the time, as you'd expect, but you might
be lucky enough to experience a three-courser like lobster
and truffle ravioli with savoy cabbage and shellfish
cream to start, pot roast pork cheek with char-grilled
langoustine and honey roast vegetables as a main, and
Armagnac parfait with poached pear as dessert. The
sheer amount of craft displayed is phenomenal.

The Waterfront

1C Dock Place (554 7427). Bus 1, 16, 22, 35, 36, 49.
Meals served noon-10pm daily. **Average** ££. **Credit**
AmEx, MC, V.
Established back in 1982, the Waterfront remains a class
act. Like many of its nearby competitors, it has a wood-
panelled, sea-themed bar, with booth seating, a bright,
open conservatory and even a mini floating dock where
people can sit in summer. The wine list is pretty good
(and lengthy) and some customers come just to sip a
bottle of red and munch olives for an hour or two. The
kitchen can also provide a three-course meal: say, pan-
fried squid with chorizo and olives to start, followed by
halibut with mussel and saffron sauce, then crème brûlée
with lavender shortbread. There's also a specials menu
that goes from the sublime (half a lobster with hazelnut
and coriander butter) to the not so sublime (beetroot and
sweet potato samosa). Despite the odd vegetarian lapse
of judgement, this is still a fine establishment.

Zinc Bar & Grill

Ocean Terminal Shopping Mall, Victoria Dock (553 8070/
www.conran-restaurants.co.uk). Bus 11, 22, 35, 36, 49.
Meals served noon-10pm Mon-Thur; noon-11pm Fri-
Sun. **Average** £££. **Credit** AmEx, DC, MC, V.
Ocean Terminal is a shopping mall. It may be a
cavernous, designer edifice that resembles a cruise liner,
with a cinema and the retired Royal Yacht *Britannia*
berthed outside, but it's still a shopping mall. It's about
half a mile west from the main cluster of Leith restaurants

Crombie's
(97-101
Broughton
Street, 557
0111) for
meat! This
butcher
makes
fabulous
haggis and
prize-winning
sausages.

and bars, so unless a session of waterfront retail therapy makes you ravenous, you're really going to have to intend to come to its flagship eaterie: Terence Conran's Zinc Bar & Grill. Big, modern, with excellent views, it's the only Conran restaurant in Scotland. The menu is very flexible; you can just have some falafel, tabouleh and flatbread, with a beer, or a full three-course experience. That could mean starting with prawn wun tun or fried whitebait; moving on to a New York sirloin steak with harissa sauce; and finishing with a neat chocolate pot. The cooking is efficient and the restaurant tries hard to add atmosphere (DJs at the weekend), but you can't help wondering if it would all have worked better in the city centre. There's also an attached café-bar, Ocean Kitchen & Ocean Bar.

Scottish

No.3 Royal Terrace
3 Royal Terrace (477 4747/www.no3royalterrace.com). Playhouse buses. **Meals served** noon-2pm, 5.30-10pm daily. **Average** £££. **Credit** AmEx, DC, MC, V.
This restaurant gives the impression of being off the beaten track, but it's only a two-minute stroll from busy

The Italian job

In among all the various eating out choices in Edinburgh, there are three cuisines that stand head and shoulders above the rest in terms of restaurant numbers. Chinese, Indian and, most of all, Italian.

From the very formal end of the scale such as **Santini** (*see p123*) through to modern national chains like **Pizza Express** and homely neighbourhood eateries such as **Piatto Verde** (for both, *see p121*), Edinburgh has taken Italian-style food to heart. Glasgow is much the same.

Maybe that's because Italian was the first immigrant cuisine to hit central Scotland in modern times and has had more than 100 years to

work its magic. Italy was economically depressed in the late 19th century, and into the 20th, so Italians sought alternative destinations. The cities of the US were one route, of course, but so also were Edinburgh and Glasgow.

Once in Scotland, the newcomers looked for small business opportunities – and that's the simple explanation for the number of ice-cream parlours and fish and chip shops with an Italian ring to their names. Edinburgh's best chippie is **L'Alba d'Oro** for example (5 Henderson Row, 557 2580, Stockbridge), while **Luca's**, just east of Edinburgh in the little coastal town of Musselburgh, is an

Leith Walk. Housed in a distinguished row of Georgian buildings on Calton Hill, the interior has a mix of styles, from cornices and chandeliers to tartan carpet and robust wooden furniture. There's a sociable eating space in the bar downstairs and a more polite restaurant room upstairs. Most of the wine list is under £20 and the menu offers a wide choice: salmon and dill fish cake on spinach to start is competent, while a vegetarian main such as parmesan tart filled with char-grilled Mediterranean vegetables is very good indeed. Diners can also choose pasta, salads or fish, but grilled fine cuts of Scotch beef are the signature dishes. Presentation of desserts is accomplished and the service is upbeat. Eclectic on several levels, but it all meshes together somehow.

Café-bars & Cafés

Baroque
39-41 Broughton Street (557 0627). Bus 8, 17, Playhouse buses. **Open** 10am-1am daily. **Meals served** 10am-10pm daily. **Average** £. **Credit** AmEx, MC, V.

old-fashioned café where the gelato is made next door (34 High Street, 665 2237). It also has a branch in South Edinburgh (16 Morningside Road, 446 0233).

But it wasn't all scoops of vanilla and fish suppers. The roots of **Valvona & Crolla** (*see p91*), a wonderful delicatessen and caffè bar, go back to the 1890s, when Benedetto Valvona, who hailed from Cassino in central Italy, sold Italian food and wine in the Old Town. His son Raffaele took over from him, then went into business with one Alfonso Crolla in 1934, setting up shop on Elm Row, off Leith Walk – where you'll find it still trading today.

As the 20th century progressed, the Italian community diversified – there is a limit to the number of chippers and ice-cream shops you can have in such a small country. First came relatively inexpensive trattorias and pizzerias, some of which have now lasted for decades and, like the **Jolly Pizzeria** (*see p81*), provided an affordable sit-down experience to a section of society that would never have eaten out in a restaurant before. Nowadays, Italian establishments in Edinburgh provide everything from a posh night out to a quick panini and lager.

For all this, Scotland owes a debt of gratitude. *Grazie.*

A decor compromise makes Baroque a barometer of changing mores. When it opened a few years ago, it was a 1990s riot of confused styles (Matisse prints, cracked tile cladding on the pillars, bright colours). A refurb has calmed it down a little, but you can't disguise the queasy metallic curves of the bar frontage or the odd flash of flamboyance that's survived. All the same, it's open to the street in summer, serves all the basic booze choices and the menu makes an effort to be at least a little interesting. That means the all-day breakfast options include spiced kedgeree with coriander eggs, as well as the standard fry-up, while salads encompass Thai beef and a typical pasta dish would be linguine with almond and oregano pesto. In the evenings, Baroque functions much more as a pre-club bar, so don't expect a quiet night.

Bar Sirius

7-10 Dock Place (555 3344). Bus 1, 16, 22, 35, 36, 49.
Open 11.30am-midnight Mon-Wed, Sun; 11.30am-1am Thur-Sat. **Meals served** noon-9pm Mon-Thur, Sat, Sun; noon-4pm Fri. **Average** £. **Credit** MC, V.
Café-bars could be said to be defined by a certain self-consciousness about their style. Bar Sirius certainly has that with its rough orange walls and designer-ish chairs, a look that has endured for some years now. It's not quite as smart as it used to be, but it's a fine place to meet friends, hang out, drink wine or lager, and snack. On Saturdays and Sundays, you can get brunch (full-on fried breakfasts as well as the likes of eggs florentine), while the standard menu offers soup, nachos, ciabattas and a wide selection of tapas. On nights when the DJs are strutting their stuff, there can be quite an atmosphere.

The Basement

10A-12A Broughton Street (557 0097/www.thebasement. org.uk). Bus 8, 17, Playhouse buses. **Open** noon-1am daily. **Meals served** noon-10.30pm daily. **Average** £. **Credit** AmEx, MC, V.
The original Broughton Street style bar, this place still has an orange and blue decor and eccentric furniture made from old engineering bits and bobs. The bar itself separates the establishment into two: one side is more pubby (the best draught beers are Grolsch and Deuchars IPA); the other has tables for sit-down dining. Either way, it's dark (it's a basement), atmospheric and can get pretty party-like in the evenings. You can certainly snack and the kitchen has a good reputation for its Thai dishes on Wednesdays and Mexican ones at the weekends, but there's more on offer than that. On other nights you might find pear and stilton salad to start, butternut squash with wild mushroom risotto as a main, and pecan pie with cream to finish. Conclusion: still hip, after all these years.

The Pond. *See p95.*

Blue Moon Café

36 Broughton Street (556 2788). Bus 8, 17, Playhouse buses. **Open** 11am-11.30pm Mon-Fri; 10am-11.30pm Sat, Sun. **Meals served** 11am-10.30pm daily. **Average** £. **Credit** MC, V.

At the heart of Edinburgh's pink triangle, this gay-run but straight-friendly café-bar is a popular meeting and eating place both during the dog days of midweek and at evenings towards the weekend, when the atmosphere steps up to accommodate the high spirits of the clubbing brigade. The food tends to be of the simple and filling variety (macaroni cheese, nachos, vegetarian haggis, assorted burgers, big cakes), there are some good bottled beers, economy wines and a nice book and accessories shop in the basement. If you want to know anything about the city's gay scene, ask the waiting staff who are friendly and (usually) happy to help.

The Lost Sock

11 East London Street (557 6097). Bus 8, 13, 17. **Open** 10am-9.30pm Mon-Sat; 10am-5pm Sun. **Average** £. **No credit cards**.

A small, contemporary-looking café attached to a dry-cleaner and launderette – it's a wonder no one thought of doing this before, or again. Certainly, the idea of having a bottle of Stella or Budvar (and a plate of deep-fried squid, perhaps) while you're waiting for your laundry to finish is pretty tempting. The food's interesting enough even to draw in people who own washing machines; the menu, chalked up on several boards across one wall, is immense. The all-day breakfast choices include huevos rancheros; there are also baguettes, wraps, vegetarian main meals (old-fashioned macaroni cheese, for instance), chicken or steak stir-fries, and much more. Drink options are limited, mind (a couple of bottled lagers and some wine), and desserts are real comforters, like dark and deadly sticky chocolate cake. When the mini bank of TV screens is working, you might get MTV. 'The Sock', as fans call it, gets very busy at weekend brunch time.

The Outhouse

12A Broughton Street Lane (557 6668). Bus 8, 17, Playhouse buses. **Open** noon-1am daily. **Meals served** noon-8pm Mon-Thur; noon-4pm Fri-Sun. **Average** £. **Credit** AmEx, DC, MC, V.

The forgotten café-bar on the Broughton Street scene. It's hidden halfway down a back lane and doesn't look as cared for as it once did, but there are still flowers on the bar, a dark wood and stone floor, food, and Guinness and Stella Artois on tap. The functional menu offers baked potatoes, club sandwiches, burgers, wraps and salads, plus more substantial Mexican dishes such as burritos, chimichangas and quesadillas. But the main attraction is that you can sit outside; there's a beer garden at the back with green picnic tables and white awnings that looks oddly like a July wedding in Surrey. No views, though: it's enclosed by surrounding buildings and there's a wall of graffiti as a design feature (not exactly like that Surrey wedding then). If on some summer's day the pavement tables at Baroque (*see p87*) or PopRokit (*see p95*) round the corner are taken, try here.

Sugo

14-15 Albert Place, Leith Walk (554 7282). Bus 7, 10, 12, 14, 16, 22, 25, 49. **Open** 11am-11pm Mon-Thur, Sun; 11am-1am Fri, Sat. **Meals served** 11am-11pm Mon-Thur, Sun; 11am-10.30pm Fri, Sat. **Average** £. **Credit** MC, V.

When Sugo opened in 2002, halfway down Leith Walk, a lot of people in the neighbourhood gave thanks. At last, somewhere they could go for a glass of wine and some food without having to head to the city centre, or the heart of Leith down by the Shore. Sugo is on the ground floor of a tenement block, but has been adapted well with lilies on the bar, a grey and purple decor, sofas and the odd glass brick. Yes, you can just get a drink (short wine list, basic beers like Guinness or Stella on tap), but the menu is pretty extensive. Breakfast lasts until noon, lunch until 5pm and dinner till 11pm; the ambitious evening list has everything from pizza, pasta and steaks to alcoholic milkshakes. You're sure to find something that takes your fancy if you've been working through a bottle of red.

The top of Leith Walk, by the Playhouse Theatre, is one of the city's gay centres. Bars include **Planet Out** (6 Baxter's Place, 524 0061) and **Café Habana** (22 Greenside Place, 558 1270).

Port O'Leith. *See p96.*

Valvona & Crolla Caffè Bar ★

19 Elm Row, off Leith Walk (556 6066/www.valvona crolla.com). Bus 7, 10, 12, 14, 16, 22, 25, 49. **Open** 8am-6.30pm daily. **Meals served** 8am-6pm daily. **Average** ££. **Credit** AmEx, MC, V.

Valvona & Crolla is the best delicatessen in Scotland, and one of the best in the whole UK. Its café-bar is a simple and tasteful space at the rear of the shop, a former stable block, with white walls and wooden beams. The food draws on the quality of raw materials sold in the deli (shipped in fresh from Italian markets). Take breakfast, for instance. Options include paesano sausage with smoked bacon, fried egg, grilled polenta, tomato and bread; or panettone in carrozza (sweet brioche dipped in egg, fried, and served with cream). The flavoursome verdure breakfast involves grilled courgette, red pepper, aubergine and cherry tomato, a fried egg, polenta and mushrooms. Later in the day, the regular menu offers salads, snacks like bruschetta, and excellent panatella sandwiches (such as gorgonzola, roasted courgette, pine kernels and rocket). The more substantial specials (meat, fish, pizza) change on a daily basis, and there's a great selection of Italian wines too. Peerless.

Pubs & Bars

The Barony

81-83 Broughton Street (557 0546/www.baronybar.co.uk). Bus 8, 17, Playhouse buses. **Open** 11am-12.30am Mon-Sat; 12.30-11pm Sun. **Credit** AmEx, DC, MC, V.

This is a very traditional looking pub, with brewery mirrors and distressed wood everywhere. It has cask ales (Caledonian 80/-, Deuchars IPA) and sometimes guest rarities such as Auld Scoop from the Houston Brewery in Renfrewshire; it offers a full menu of basic pub grub as well as breakfast on Sunday afternoons; the whisky choice is adequate; and there's live music on Sunday nights (often two guys with acoustic guitars). The atmosphere wouldn't be entirely out of place in one of the neighbouring style bars, though, in terms of clientele and buzz – the crowd has a slightly younger (and more gender-mixed) profile than your average boozer. For rare ales and football on the TV, walk down a few doors and visit the Cask & Barrel (*see below*).

Cask & Barrel ★

115 Broughton Street (556 3132). Bus 8, 17, Playhouse buses. **Open** 11am-12.30am Mon-Wed; 11am-1am Thur-Sat; 12.30pm-12.30am Sun. **Credit** AmEx, MC, V.

Although the layout is different, with a big horseshoe bar in the middle of the room, there are plenty of superficial similarities between the Cask & Barrel and the Barony (*see above*) just up the street: brewery mirrors, wooden fixtures and fittings, and cask ales. But look closer and you'll see that this is much more of a drinks specialist than its neighbour: beer heaven, in effect. As well as the local brews (Caledonian 80/- and Deuchars IPA from Edinburgh), there are also English beers on tap (Flowers, Timothy Taylor's Landlord, Bass) and really obscure Scottish artisan examples (Cowie from the Borders, or Ice Maiden from Harviestoun, for instance). The bottled beers include around a dozen from Germany and the Low Countries, and wherever you are in the bar, you'll be able to see one of the TV screens, often showing the footie. Bar food is on offer at lunchtime, and basic filled rolls and toasties the rest of the time.

Scotland's leading outdoors shop is **Graham Tiso**. Its huge branch in Leith (41 Commercial Street, 554 0804) now has a nifty café in among the walking boots and sleeping bags.

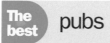

The best pubs

For whisky lovers
The small but beautifully formed **Bow Bar** (*see p47*) has a large but beautifully formed selection of whiskies – as does **Kay's** (*see p72*). Or there's the **Scotch Malt Whisky Society Members' Room** (*see p97*), but you have to become a member first.

For beer lovers
Ales aplenty at the **Cask & Barrel** (*see p92*) and **Starbank Inn** (*see p98*) in Leith, the **Guildford Arms** (*see p72*) in the New Town, and the **Bow Bar** (*see p47*) in the Old Town.

For music lovers
Folk fans should head to **Sandy Bell's** (*see p47*); rock fans to **Whistle Binkies** (*see p48*). And you can also have a drink at music shop **FOPP** (*see p71*).

King's Wark
36 The Shore (554 9260). Bus 1, 16, 22, 35, 36, 49. **Open** noon-11pm Mon-Thur; noon-midnight Fri, Sat; 11am-11pm Sun. **Credit** MC, V.
When is a pub not a pub? The crossover between restaurants, café-bars and drinking dens in Edinburgh these days can be a little baffling, and the standard of cooking at the King's Wark is certainly good. But when you walk in, it looks like a bar (neat, wood-clad, candlelit in the evenings and cosy) that just happens to have a small ante-room for dining purposes. Aside from the classic haddock in beer batter and chips, you could also have a proper three-course meal: perhaps pan-fried red snapper to start, followed by fillet of halibut with lemon butter sauce as a main, and polished off with plum sponge. Cask ales on offer include the Wildcat (from Tomintoul in the Scottish Highlands) and Deuchars IPA from Edinburgh. All very different from the branch of Pizza Express next door.

Noble's
44A Constitution Street (554 2024). Bus 16, 35. **Open** 11am-midnight Mon-Wed, Sun; 11am-1am Thur-Sat. **Credit** MC, V.
Noble's changes its face depending on the time of day. Catch it at a weekday lunchtime and Leith office staff will be tucking into bar food such as nachos, fishermen's

pasta or cumberland sausage. On Friday and Saturday
nights, it has live music. On a quiet afternoon, there's time
to sit and watch the light flood through the stained-glass
windows (with ship motif), and realise that the plants by
the toilet give the space a slightly raffish look. If – on that
quiet afternoon – there's introspective indie on the sound
system and the malt of the moment is a Springbank, then
you've got all the makings for a bit of soul-searching. In
essence though, this is a classic, well-kept, wood 'n'
leather bar. It aims for a new guest cask ale every week
(Timothy Taylor's Landlord, for example) to go with
regulars (Caledonian 80/- and Deuchars IPA).

Old Chain Pier ★

32 Trinity Crescent (552 1233). Bus 10, 11, 16, 32.
Open 11am-11pm Mon-Wed; 11am-midnight Thur-Sat;
12.30-11pm Sun. **Credit** MC, V.
This could be the bar with everything. It may be out of
the way – in the suburb of Trinity in the north of the city
– but it's always worth a detour. For a start, the Old Chain
Pier is literally perched on the sea wall; on wild nights
when there's a high tide and the wind is up, spray even
flecks the windows. (No surprises at the ship's cabin
decor then.) The cask ale is well cared for, with usually
five on offer, including the likes of Burton, Adnams and
Timothy Taylor's Landlord. And the food is just great:

The Barony.
See p92.

vegetable tempura, 'Trinity chowder', French lamb stew, ribeye steak and more (although it's a small kitchen, so don't expect speed miracles). Watch the ships pass along the Forth by day and the lights flickering on the Fife coast at night; even the occasional heron. As Edinburgh pub experiences go, hard to beat.

Pivo Caffè

2-6 Calton Road (557 2925). Bus 30, 40. **Open** 4pm-3am daily. **Credit** MC, V.

Pivo is tucked away down Calton Road, no distance at all from the east end of Princes Street. Although it has a Czech theme, and the lagers to go with it (Gambrinus, Krusovice, Staropramen and more), the main selling point is that it's a late-night DJ bar: the DJ booth is busy from when the bar opens in the late afternoon right through to closing time at 3am. And these aren't just wannabes either; some of the spinners (especially Thursday to Saturday) are well known on the Scottish scene. There are velvet benches and leather sofas to sit on, wooden tables, a low ceiling, assorted posters in a style you'll remember from your trip to Prague, and lots of noise and atmosphere once things pick up.

The Pond

2 Bath Road (467 3825). Bus 12, 16, 35, 36. **Open** 4pm-1am Tue-Thur; 1pm-1am Fri-Sun. **No credit cards**.

It looks like the pub at the end of the universe, in an unlovely street between Leith Links and the docks (single women might find the walk here intimidating in the dark) – and the Pond is never going to win any design prizes. It resembles a hand-knitted university common room dumped in the middle of nowhere, with an interior decor that probably started as a good idea then got abandoned as too much bother (the fish theme through the back, for instance). That said, if you get a pint of German wheat beer, a bag of bombay mix and slump in one of the front-of-house sofas, the Pond can seem like a home from home. It's unique, it can be a little cliquey, but if you got lost on the east side of Leith you'd be glad to find it.

PopRokit

2 Picardy Place (556 4272). Bus 8, 10, 11, 15, 17, 21, 44. **Open** 11am-1am daily. **Credit** MC, V.

PopRokit was originally called the Catwalk and appeared in 1997. At the time it was a major departure; while every other style bar in the city was painted blue and orange, with wrought-iron furniture, it went for bare concrete minimalism on two floors. That hasn't changed, so the place still stands out, although it's not quite as fresh as it used to be. During the day, people drop in for coffee, drinks and snacks, but it's much more of a pre-club bar in the evening, with DJs downstairs at weekends. You

The Village. *See p98.*

can get Scrumpy Jack or Pilsner Urquell on tap, bottled fruit beers or order a cocktail (Cocaine Martini; a standard martini with framboise). On the food front, there are various breakfast options, panini and a range of combos (sesame crusted pork with honey and red pepper, for example) that you can have as a salad, in ciabatta or in pitta. In summer, the pavement tables are a great place to watch a busy world go by.

Port O'Leith ★

58 Constitution Street (554 3568/www.portoleith.co.uk).
Bus 16, 35. **Open** 8.30am-1am Mon-Sat; 12.30pm-1am
Sun. **No credit cards.**

A legend. You could sit here for an hour before you even talked to anyone, working out the details: ships' flags on the ceiling, lifebelts, snuff for sale behind the bar, and a black and white linoleum floor. A tidily run 'howf' patronised by everyone from visiting merchant mariners (the docks are nearby) to locals and students experimenting with the saltier side of life. There are always fresh red paper tablecloths on the tables, little nightlights adding atmosphere – and the drinks aren't expensive. This place has more character than the entire parliamentary Labour Party; and the jukebox's not bad either (in a classic Tina Turner or the Animals kind of way). Essence of Leith.

Need a sandwich? **Fleur's Deli** in Leith (52 The Shore, 554 8841) makes very good ones.

Robbie's

367 Leith Walk (554 6850). Bus 7, 10, 12, 14, 16, 22, 25, 49. **Open** noon-midnight Mon-Fri; 11am-midnight Sat; 12.30pm-midnight Sun. **No credit cards**.

This looks like an old man's pub that's been colonised by the younger element for years, with a cask ale interest thrown in, producing the sort of eclecticism that sees club and indie gig posters all over the walls of what would otherwise be an unadorned boozer. There's still an element of *Trainspotting* about Robbie's that gives it an interest other (unwelcoming) Leith Walk pubs don't have. There are nice beers (Dark Island from Orkney, Lia Fail from Perth, Deuchars IPA from Edinburgh, Bass from Burton), a good mix of clients, and the TV shows the football and the *Simpsons*. Nothing more is required.

The Scotch Malt Whisky Society Members' Room ★

The Vaults, 87 Giles Street (555 2266). Bus 1, 7, 10, 14, 22. **Open** 10am-5pm Mon-Wed; 10am-11pm Thur, Fri; 11am-2.30pm, 5-11pm Sat. **Credit** AmEx, MC, V.

This is a private club with the distinguished look of a crusty gentlemen's haunt in central London. Fortunately, its membership encompasses a wide range of ages and both sexes, and it's the prime place in Edinburgh to drink the rarest single malt whiskies on the planet. The society buys casks of single malts from Scottish distilleries, bottles the contents and sells it to members – either by the bottle, or by the dram in the Members' Room (which also serves bottled beer and other drinks). The whisky is strong (55%-65% abv), limited in quantity – the output from each cask only runs to a few hundred bottles – and can vary from sublime to banal. As noted, the society isn't as uptight as it might look and anyone can walk in off the street and join for £40. That covers the first year, then it's £25 a year after that (and members can bring in two guests). Some winter afternoon when you're comatose in a chesterfield in the Members' Room, in front of a real fire, sipping a fabulous whisky from 'somewhere on Islay', that membership fee will seem like a bargain.

Starbank Inn

64 Laverockbank Road (552 4141). Bus 10, 11, 16, 32. **Open** 11am-11pm Mon-Wed; 11am-midnight Thur-Sat; 12.30-11pm Sun. **Credit** MC, V.

The Starbank is set back on the other side of the road from the sea wall, and raised slightly, so the views of the Firth of Forth are arguably better than from the Old Chain Pier (*see p94*) just yards away. Like the OCP, the Starbank has a reputation for good food (there's a dining conservatory attached), and it sells a good selection of Scottish cask ales, including Sandy Hunter's, St Andrew's Ale and guest rarities such as Clipper IPA from the Broughton Brewery. The decor is simple – even sparse – with lots of wood and green leather bench seats. So what's the big difference between the two pubs? This has a more patrician air. Try both and see which you prefer…

The Village

16 South Fort Street (478 7810/www.bevillage.com). *Bus 1, 7, 14.* **Open** noon-midnight Mon-Thur, Sun; noon-1am Fri, Sat. **Credit** MC, V.

To be frank, t he backstreets off the east end of Ferry Road aren't pretty – they remind you more of Irvine Welsh's *Trainspotting* than Sir Walter Scott's *Waverley*. So you might think the drinking dens would be either formulaic or too robust for the casual visitor. Not this one. Mind you, the Village isn't so much a pub as an ongoing piece of performance art by the staff; you'll find few other places in the area where they're busy debating which CD to play next: Gomez or the music from *O Brother, Where Art Thou?*. The main bar area is happily basic, while the adjacent lounge has bare stone walls, blonde wood furniture and art shows. Lunch is offered from Monday to Saturday (cashew and butternut squash soup, chicken and leek pie), and a brunch menu on Sundays (American-style pancakes, full breakfasts). The Village also hosts small gigs and theme nights.

Edinburgh: South

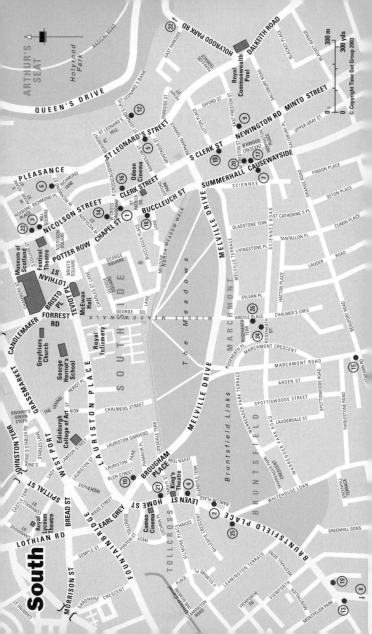

South Edinburgh encompasses some of the better-heeled parts of the city, and thus has a selection of bars and restaurants to buttress that status. Bruntsfield and Morningside in the south-west have busy main thoroughfares (Bruntsfield Place, Morningside Road) containing popular establishments, while the side streets are altogether more residential. Marchmont, south of the Meadows, is desert-like when it comes to eating and drinking – with a couple of notable exceptions – but in the south-east there are restaurants, cafés and bars near Edinburgh University's main campus, and the persistent buzz of Nicolson Street and Clerk Street (a main route into the city centre). Newington and Causewayside conceal the odd gem.

Restaurants

Asian

Ann Purna

45 St Patrick Square (662 1807). Bus 3, 5, 7, 8, 14, 29, 31, 33, 37, 49. **Meals served** noon-2pm, 5.30-11pm Mon-Fri; 5.30-11pm Sat, Sun. **Average** ££. **Credit** MC, V.
Ann Purna is one block west of Edinburgh University's precincts, has a wholly vegetarian menu and a relaxed style (although the decor may be a little bright 'n' cheesy for some). Students and their teachers love it – but the clientele is far from exclusively academic. It's a family-run business (the Pandyas) and the cooking has a

Bonsai

Gujarati and South Indian flavour. A bhel poori starter
is exactly the kind of thing you won't find in many other
allegedly Indian restaurants in Edinburgh. Or try the
patra (steamed arvi leaves deep-fried with gram flour).
Main dishes include a fine selection of toothsome daalain
(lentil stews), plus specialities such as kofta malai and
Ann Purna baingan (aubergine with nuts and onion). The
'business' lunches are ludicrously cheap, and there's
Indian lager on tap.

Ayutthaya
*14B Nicolson Street (556 9351). Nicolson Street-North
Bridge buses.* **Meals served** noon-2.30pm, 5.30-10.30pm
daily. **Average** ££. **Credit** AmEx, DC, MC, V.
Given the number of Thai restaurants that opened in the
capital in 2001 and 2002, the long-established Ayutthaya
is starting to look like an elder statesman on the scene.

It's a relatively small establishment and although it won't win any design awards, it is handy for the Festival Theatre opposite and offers pre- and post-theatre menus. Familiar Thai dishes are on offer, but it's worth exploring a little off the beaten track in taste terms. Gai yang – a whole, small chicken marinated in honey and spices, grilled over charcoal and served with a sweet chilli sauce – is one example. There's also a vegetarian menu, a choice of set banquets (also with a vegetarian option) or, if all you want is good old tom yum soup, then green curry with chicken, that's available too.

Branch: Sukhothai 23 Brougham Place, West (229 1537).

Bonsai

46 West Richmond Street (668 3847/www.bonsaibar bistro.co.uk). Nicolson Street-North Bridge buses. **Meals served** noon-9pm Mon-Fri; 1-9pm Sat; 5-9pm Sun. **Average** £. **Credit** MC, V.

For many, Edinburgh's Japanese restaurant scene would seem to be dominated by the high-profile southern intruder Yo! Sushi (*see p55*) from London. Fortunately, a rising Scottish chef, Andrew Ramage, decided to create his own chemical, Nipponese-flavoured bistro. Bonsai is friendly, not formulaic and nestles quietly in a Southside backstreet, with a Japanese team in the kitchen producing dishes that won't spook the Scots palate. There's assorted tempura and user-friendly maki sushi with such fillings as avocado and red pepper or avocado, tuna and mayonnaise. But if you want roast eel nigiri sushi, tart umeboshi plums and some (raw) squid sashimi, that's available too. Vegetarians have no problem – try shiitake mushroom yakitori or daikon salad with roasted seaweed.

Dragon Way

74-78 South Clerk Street (668 1328). Bus 3, 5, 7, 8, 14, 29, 31, 33, 37, 49. **Meals served** noon-2.30pm, 5pm-midnight daily. **Average** ££. **Credit** AmEx, DC, MC, V.

Ornamentation is not a word that crops up in food guides very often, but then there are few places like Dragon Way. This restaurant has gilded birds and dragons on the walls, another lacquer dragon wrapped around a column, a small waterfall and other elaborate design features. The menu's good too, with Peking, Sichuan and Cantonese cooking as well as seafood specialities. That could mean anything from king prawns lar chee (cooked with mixed vegetables, rice wine and chilli) to chicken cheung bau (marinated, then stir-fried, with yellow bean sauce), as well as mainstays like beef chow mein, sweet and sour pork or crispy duck. Seafood depends on the catch of the day, but a typical dish would be sea bass with ginger,

Dragon Way.
See p103.

spring onion, coriander and fish sauce. Presentation rates highly and a night with friends at one of Dragon Way's big round tables is an experience on several levels.

Kalpna ★

2-3 St Patrick Square (667 9890). Bus 3, 5, 7, 8, 14, 29, 31, 33, 37, 49. **Meals served** noon-2.30pm, 5.30-11pm Mon-Sat; 5.30-11pm Sun. **Average** £. **Credit** MC, V.

The more self-consciously vegetarian of the city's two veggie Indian restaurants (nearby Ann Purna is the other; *see p101*), Kalpna has been plying its trade since the 1980s. The continuous stream of happy, chatty diners is testament to its enduring popularity, and the menu is far from subcontinental cliché. Proof? You could start with aloo firdoshi (potatoes stuffed with pistachio, raisins, coriander and spices) or hara kebab (fried spinach and green peas stuffed with saffron yoghurt). The thali options give a nice spread of dishes as an alternative to starter/main/sides, but some specialities and traditional offerings on the menu are just dandy in themselves. Waiters can advise on wine, and there's Indian lager on tap and some overwhelmingly sweet puds.

Namaste

41-42 West Preston Street (466 7061). Bus 3, 5, 7, 8, 29, 31, 37, 42, 49. **Meals served** 5.30pm-11pm daily. **Average** £. **Credit** MC, V.

What Namaste has going for it isn't so much the food, although that's decent enough: a fair-sized menu of robust if predictable dishes such as pakora, fish tikka, rogan josh or jalfrezi lamb, and the odd unexpected offering like machli Amritsari (red snapper in spiced gravy) and dahl mahkni (black lentil stew). Nor does Namaste stand out because everything seems to come in a little brass pot. A North Indian frontier theme and distressed wooden fixtures help, but it really scores because it twists your

Stromboli (20 Bruntsfield Place, 229 7247) is a café/takeaway that does excellent pies: puff pastry filled with assorted stir-fries.

head. Despite arriving on the scene in 2001, it looks like a ramshackle hippie conception of India from the time the Rolling Stones were recording *Beggars Banquet*. Meanwhile, the background music sounds like Bollywood meets Massive Attack. An experience.

Suruchi

14A Nicolson Street (556 6583). Buses 3, 7, 14, 21, 29, 31, 33. **Meals served** noon-2pm, 5.30-11pm Mon-Sat; 5.30-11pm Sun. **Average** £. **Credit** AmEx, DC, MC, V.
Easily one of the best Indian restaurants in Edinburgh, Suruchi distinguishes itself with regular food festivals, an eclectic menu (written in Scots) and because it actually makes an effort – all appreciated by its clientele. Yes, there's pakora and chicken kebab among the starters but also South Indian offerings like bonda (potato dumplings with raisins and spices in gram flour). Conservative diners might stick to tried-and tested mains (lamb jalfrezi, tandoori king prawns) or they could opt for nirvana: chicken with lemongrass, mustard seeds, curry leaves, lemon and coconut. There's also a 'hame produce' section drawing on key ingredients of the Scottish larder, including salmon chi kori (salmon with black pepper, ginger, spices and coconut) and tandoori trout (whole trout cooked in the tandoor, served with salad and rice). **Branch**: **Suruchi Too** 121 Constitution Street, North-east & Leith (554 3268).

Thai Lemongrass

40-41 Bruntsfield Place (229 2225). Bus 11, 15, 16, 17, 23, 45. **Meals served** 5-11.30pm Mon-Thur; noon-11.30pm Fri-Sun. **Average** ££. **Credit** AmEx, MC, V.
One of a new wave of Thai restaurants, Thai Lemongrass arrived in late 2002 and was praised from the outset. It's spacious enough, with uplifting yellow walls and dark wooden furniture. There are set banquets for two to three people or four to seven; there's also a short vegetarian menu for those wanting to avoid the fish, chicken or pork involved in most other dishes. Although there are lots of seafood choices and grilled meats (including duck and lamb), the menu also has soups, salads (spicy green papaya with shrimp, chilli, peanuts, tomato and tamarind sauce) and wok dishes (stir-fried chicken and dry chilli with mushroom and cashew). Desserts are basic, but this is one of the city's better Thai establishments.

Thaisanuk ★

21 Argyle Place (221 1231/www.thaisanuk.com). Bus 24, 41. **Meals served** 6-11pm daily. **Average** ££. **Credit** DC, MC, V.
A tiny restaurant in a baronial suburb south of the Meadows, Thaisanuk has the kind of winning attitude that captures hearts and minds – so book ahead; it can

get very busy and doesn't have much space. The menu is simple: starters, mains and noodles. Fresh ingredients are shipped in from as far afield as Thailand itself, giving the traditional tom yum soup (with lemongrass, galangal and lime leaves) an extra zing. Other starters include Indonesian spare ribs and Vietnamese spring rolls. Noodles, whether dry bowls or soups, are pretty generous and come in various versions from all over Asia (Vietnamese, Malaysian, Japanese, Korean). For mains there are dishes like Asian barbecue sticks (meat or tofu with salad and sticky rice) or whole sea bass marinated in Thai basil, served with crisped skin and a lime and sweet basil sauce. It gets the popular vote as Edinburgh's best Thai restaurant.

Modern European

The Apartment ★
7-13 Barclay Place (228 6456). Bus 11, 15, 16, 17, 23, 45. **Meals served** 5.45-11pm Mon-Fri; noon-3pm, 5.45-11pm Sat, Sun. **Average** ££. **Credit** MC, V.
The Apartment arrived in autumn 1999 and *le tout Edimbourg* fell instantly in love with its minimalism, menu and super-hip staff. Its success leans on the food, but its status as a canteen for middle-class hipsters owes a lot to location: the upmarket areas of Bruntsfield, Merchiston and Marchmont are right on the doorstep. Key dishes are 'chunky healthy lines', known as CHLs (char-grilled chunks on a skewer, served with ample amounts of pitta and coleslaw), and 'slabs' (thick, crunchy home-made bread with 'stuff'). A typical CHL would come with North African spicy lamb balls, merguez and basil-wrapped goat's cheese, while a slab might entail melted gruyère, honey roasted ham, cracked black pepper and sweet mustard. It's a riot of flavour – but if it's not your thing, there are also salads, grilled fish, steaks and pasta. Its Old Town sister, the Outsider, which opened in autumn 2002, is much bigger and has more obvious design values, but the menu is the same.
Branch: **The Outsider** George IV Bridge, Old Town (226 3131).

Blonde
75 St Leonard's Street (668 2917). Bus 2, 21. **Meals served** 6-10pm Mon; noon-2.30pm, 6-10pm Tue-Sun. **Average** ££. **Credit** AmEx, DC, MC, V.
Blonde (so-called because of its light wood interior) is right next door to Holyrood Park and ideal if you want a relaxed meal in a nicely contemporary environment. It's been keeping the locals happy since its 2000 debut. Although it's hardly a Scottish restaurant per se, simple local ingredients are given the modern treatment and

Namaste. *See p104.*

turned into such interesting starters as pheasant and black pudding terrine with date and banana chutney, or mussels with coconut milk, lime and basil. A typical main would be braised venison jardinière cooked with root vegetables, white wine and whole peppercorns. The desserts are fun though less inspired, the wine list brief and the waitresses sharp as a tack.

Howies

208 Bruntsfield Place (221 1777). Bus 11, 15, 16, 17, 23, 45. **Meals served** noon-2.30pm, 6-10pm daily. **Average** ££. **Credit** AmEx, DC, MC, V.

Branches of Howies seem more ubiquitous than they actually are; there were only four in the city at last count, but they certainly fill a niche. It's the kind of place that young couples might use for an economical Friday night out, or where mums and dads take their university student kids for a relaxed Sunday lunch. The tables are big and wooden, and the walls bright with the odd bit of art. It's a formula, but more artisan than mass market, so all power to them. Scottish produce forms the foundation of the set menus (there's no à la carte) – but only the foundation – and is forged into the likes of tian of crab, avocado and lime with cardamom syrup as a starter; Scotch beef casserole with wild mushrooms, shallots and marjoram as a main; and dark chocolate and Drambuie tart to finish. The Bruntsfield Place branch is housed in a former bank and is perhaps the quirkiest of the four. **Branches**: 10-14 Victoria Street, Old Town (225 1721); 4 Glanville Place, Kerr Street, New Town & Stockbridge (225 5553); 29 Waterloo Place, North-east & Leith (556 5766).

Popular chain **Howies** has three other branches: the Victoria Street one is cosy and Old Townish; Glanville Place is a decent local eaterie; and Waterloo Place, the biggest, offers space and light.

Ann Purna
One of two vegetarian Indians, and a happy family place. *See p101.*

Bann UK
No David Bann these days, but still a cut above the opposition. *See p28.*

David Bann
Out on his own in all senses: currently the city's finest vegetarian restaurant. *See p28.*

Engine Shed
Wholesome snacks, and support for adults with learning difficulties. *See p110.*

Henderson's
The classic veggie canteen since the 1960s. *See p64.*

Kalpna
Exclusively vegetarian Indian; popular and well established. *See p104.*

Legume
A French-style vegetarian restaurant? *Sacre bleu!* But *pas demi-mauvais*, as they say around here. *See p24.*

Black Bo's
The one that decided to start serving meat – but still veggie in temperament. *See p28.*

Marque ★

19 Causewayside (466 6660). Bus 3, 5, 7, 8, 29, 31, 37, 42, 49. **Meals served** 11.45am-2pm, 5.30-10pm Wed, Thur; 11.45am-2pm, 5.30-11pm Fri; noon-2pm, 5.30-11pm Sat; noon-2pm, 5.30-10pm Sun. **Average** £££. **Credit** AmEx, MC, V.
The Marque isn't a great trumpet-blowing example of restaurant bombast. It's neat, has an understated class and does its thing quite quietly at its original premises in Causewayside. It's very modern/international: a typical three-course meal might start with sea bass tempura, vine tomatoes and warm smoked salmon crostini, move on to corn-fed chicken with crispy ham, parsley mash and choucroute garni, then finish with iced passionfruit and mango parfait, with pineapple sauce and coconut tuile.

Local opinion has the Marque among Edinburgh's top dozen restaurants – local opinion is right. The younger Marque Central (more central, obviously, and next door to the Lyceum Theatre) hits the same high standards, and offers good-value pre- and post-theatre menus.

Branch: Marque Central 30B Grindlay Street, West (229 9859).

Sweet Melinda's

11 Roseneath Street (229 7953). Bus 24, 41. **Meals served** 7-10pm Mon; noon-2pm, 7-10pm Tue-Sat. Closed 2wks Jan. **Average** ££. **Credit** MC, V.

Edinburgh's baronial tenement suburb of Marchmont is short on dining options, so this is an oasis in the desert. It's a bright, compact establishment with friendly-casual service and although it doesn't bill itself as a fish restaurant, there's certainly a good choice for fish lovers (and always something for vegetarians too). First-time diners tend to walk in with little expectation and walk out with a smile because of the standard of cooking. Typical starters are Thai fish cakes with sweet dipping sauce or black pudding with plum tomato and pear chutney. Mains weigh in with dishes such as pan-fried fillets of red snapper and sea bream with langoustine, clams and cockles, in a fennel, Pernod and pepper sauce; or roast cod with smoked haddock kedgeree. Basic desserts (lemon tart or sticky toffee pud) round off what you might call a real happy meal.

Café-bars & Cafés

Borough

72-80 Causewayside (668 2255/www.edin-borough.co.uk). Bus 3, 5, 7, 8, 29, 31, 37, 42, 49. **Open** *Bar* 11am-1am Mon-Sat; 12.30pm-1am Sun. **Meals served** noon-10pm Mon-Thur, Sun; noon-11pm Fri, Sat. **Average** ££. **Credit cards** AmEx, MC, V.

Borough only opened in 2001 and it's around a mile south of Princes Street, so, in Edinburgh terms, a little out of the way. Sometimes those who live outside the immediate neighbourhood have to pinch themselves as a reminder it's there. It's a very smart, contemporary boutique hotel with bar and restaurant designed by the award-winning Ben Kelly, and occupies a similar niche to the likes of Rick's (*see p68*). The large bar is good for lounging and snacking (steak and chips with peppercorn sauce, nachos, dim sum with sweet chilli sauce, or perhaps just a cocktail or beer). The separate restaurant has even more design pzazz. Three courses could involve a starter of game terrine with apple and grape chutney, followed by

Got the nacho nibbles? Then head for Mexican deli **Lupe Pinto's** (24 Leven Street, 228 6241, www. lupepintos. com). It sells everything from tequila to excellent tortilla chips.

scallops and king prawns on lemongrass skewers with vanilla risotto and curried coconut sauce, and nicely finished off by strawberry cheesecake with blood orange sorbet. Worth a trip south of the Meadows.

The Chatterbox

1 East Preston Street (667 9406). Bus 3, 5, 7, 8, 14, 29, 31, 33, 37, 49. **Open** 8.30am-5pm Mon, Tue, Thur-Sat; 11am-5pm Sun. **No credit cards**.

Empires have fallen, Scotland has gained its own parliament, but the Chatterbox endures. This small, traditional – dare one say frilly? – tearoom has a strong core of regular locals as well as visitors from the nearby Commonwealth swimming pool and student residences. Although there are simple hot dishes such as pasta, baked potatoes and a bargain all-day breakfast, it's really an ideal venue for a scone or cake and a pot of tea in the old-fashioned style.

Engine Shed

19 St Leonard's Lane (662 0040). Bus 2, 21. **Open** 10.30am-3.30pm Mon-Thur; 10.30am-2.30pm Fri. Closed 1wk Easter, 2wks July. **No credit cards**.

This vegetarian wholefood café opened in 1990 in a former maintenance shed for trains that used to run on the now defunct line out to East Lothian. It's handy for a coffee or a snack after you've hiked up, or round, Arthur's Seat. The business also involves a bakery and tofu production; the Engine Shed supplies both to shops and restaurants around the city. The main dishes on offer

Suruchi. *See p105.*

Susie's Diner
at 51-53 West Nicolson Street (667 8729) is an informal – if a tad worthy – vegetarian café close to Edinburgh University.

(cashew nut pie or spinach bake, for example) are utterly wholesome, and the bread's excellent, but what sets this enterprise apart is its training function. The full-time staff supervise adults with learning difficulties in all aspects of the work, including behind the counter. The Engine Shed may be worthy, but it's certainly worthwhile.

Human Be-In

2-8 West Crosscauseway (662 8860). Bus 7, 14, 29, 41, 42. **Open** 11am-1am daily. **Meals served** 11am-9pm daily. **Average** ££. **Credit** AmEx, MC, V.

A sharp-edged style bar close to the university, the Human Be-In is all dark wood and clean lines. There are booths to the rear for the insecure, and low, comfortable seats in front of the big windows looking out to the street. In summer you can sit outside. Although many people come here in the evening to have a lager or share a pitcher of cocktail, food is served until 9pm. That includes starters like pan-fried squid with chorizo salad and lime vinaigrette; mains such as pan-seared fillet of salmon with baby leeks, new potatoes, clams and white wine; and fresh vanilla and berry cheesecake with apricot and clove compote for dessert. It's an impressive menu and certainly a cut above the average Edinburgh café-bar, but also caters for those who just want a ciabatta sandwich.

Kaffe Politik

146-148 Marchmont Road (446 9873). Bus 24, 41. **Open** 10am-10pm daily. **Meals served** 10am-9pm daily. **No credit cards**.

Edinburgh: South

Londoners take when they go out.

London

Prior to the arrival of Kaffe Politik a few years back, Marchmont was very badly served for cafés. Now it has one of the best-looking in the city, housed in a former bank. Black and white photos of assorted politicos cover one wall and gaze balefully over the assorted students and locals as they dither over which speciality tea to have next and scan the menu. This offers paninis, pasta and noodle dishes, bagels, salads and soups – all very well done. But if there's one item that surpasses all the others it's a brunch option: scrambled eggs with Swiss cheese and chives on toast. The only drawback: the place is crowded at peak times and there aren't many tables.

Montpeliers ★

159-161 Bruntsfield Place (229 3115). Bus 11, 15, 16, 17, 23, 45. **Open** 9am-1am daily. **Meals served** 9am-10pm daily. **Average** ££. **Credit** AmEx, MC, V.

Montpeliers has been around since 1992, but the odd refurb has made sure it still looks bang up to date: clean-cut, with dark wood and subdued red lighting. The great drinks selection includes Leffe, Duvel, Arran Blonde and Anchor Steam in bottles, plus Erdinger, Hoegaarden and Deuchars IPA on tap. The cocktails are better than average too. The dining area is slightly raised, off to one side, and offers a range of dishes from breakfast, via lunch and snacks, to the full three-course evening experience. That could start with king prawns in filo with soy dip, move on to a main like Thai green chicken curry or spiced garlic lamb with coriander couscous, and finish with lime tart or Toblerone brûlée. It often gets very crowded, and it's not a space for intimate dining, but Montpeliers is among Edinburgh's top café-bars.

Ndebele

57 Home Street (221 1141/www.ndebele.co.uk). Bus 10, 11, 15, 16, 17, 23, 27, 45. **Open** 10am-10pm daily. **Average** £. **Credit** AmEx, DC, MC, V.

As the city's only African café-deli, Ndebele has foods on offer that you'd be hard pushed to find anywhere else in Edinburgh, let alone the rest of Scotland. It's a nicely scruffy, student-style hangout with staff who seem to be on a mission to bring the likes of smoked ostrich, biltong shavings and boerewors (beef sausage with coriander) to a new public. Although the general flavour is quite South African, you'll also find the likes of akara (Nigerian bean scone), falafel (a North African staple) and jollof rice (central African rice and vegetables). Soups (served with mielie bread) and more substantial hot dishes are available, but sandwiches are the mainstay; you can have just about anything you want as a filling. Vegetarians are well catered for, and if you just want something sweet to go with your coffee, try the date balls.

Pubs & Bars

Bennet's

8 Leven Street (229 5143). Bus 10, 11, 15, 16, 17, 23, 45. **Open** 11.30am-12.30am Mon-Wed; 11.30am-1am Thur-Sat; 12.30-11.30pm Sun. **Credit** MC, V.

Bennet's is a real Victorian design marvel. The long, wooden bar occupies one side of the main room, with alcoves along the top of the gantry for the huge selection of single malts (around 100), while the opposite wall has fitted red leather seats and more wooden surrounds. The tables are all glass-topped, with assorted maps providing decoration, and on nicer afternoons sunlight beams in through stained glass. There are only a couple of cask ales (McEwan's 80/-, Deuchars IPA), but the food's hearty (steak pie or macaroni cheese) and there's a room through the back if the main bar's busy. It's next door to the King's Theatre, so attracts theatre-goers before and after shows; altogether a bit of an Edinburgh classic.

The Canny Man's ★

237 Morningside Road (447 1484). Bus 11, 15, 16, 18. **Open** 11.30am-11pm Mon-Wed, Sun; 11.30am-midnight Thur, Sat; 11.30am-1am Fri. **No credit cards**.

Imagine that your family had a mad maiden aunt who was born in the Victorian era and died around the 1950s. Imagine her as a hoarder of gewgaws and oddities that she kept around the walls and ceiling of her warren-like house in prosperous Morningside. Now imagine that turned into a pub, and you've got the Canny Man's (also known as the Volunteer Arms). It's been around since 1871, has the biggest selection of single malt whisky of any Edinburgh bar, a good wine list, is pretty upmarket and offers among the most ambitious pub food in the city (half a dozen oysters or king prawns on ice, for instance, or a huge range of Danish open sandwiches, aka smørrebrød). There's a tiny beer garden, and also an attitude: the sign by the door says 'dress smart but casual' – so don't say you weren't warned. Fabulous all the same.

Cloisters

26 Brougham Street (221 9997). Bus 11, 15, 16, 17, 23, 45. **Open** 11am-midnight Mon-Thur, Sun; 11am-12.30am Fri, Sat. **No credit cards**.

Housed in a former manse, and physically attached to a church, you can see where Cloisters got its name. The decor is simple, with wood everywhere and some leather-backed bench seats that resemble upmarket pews, but it's draught beer that's the big selling point here, not cutting-edge interior design. That means Edinburgh staples like Caledonian 80/-, as well as occasional English examples

Cheesemonger extraordinaire **Iain J Mellis** has a branch of his empire at 205 Bruntsfield Place (447 8889).

seldom seen in Scotland (Greene King IPA) and some seldom seen anywhere (Dent Brewery's Aviator Ale). Nine are available at any time, and around 40 single malts.

Meadow Bar

42-44 Buccleuch Street (667 6907). Bus 41, 42. **Open** 11.30am-1am daily. **Credit** MC, V.

A student paradise round the corner from the main university buildings, Meadow has sofas for slumping, drinks promotions, cheap snack food and is slightly ramshackle. There's also an anomalous dragon sculpture above the bar. If they've got any red wine, you'll be lucky; if they don't there is an alternative: the Scottish alcoholic's beverage of choice, Buckfast tonic wine, on an optic. It's a good place to meet drunken English lit students who want to bend your ear about Martha Gellhorn's obvious superiority to that bloke Hemingway, or similar. Nice lighting effects in the garden at the back, and there is an upstairs section too.

Sheep Heid

43-45 The Causeway (656 6951). Bus 4, 42, 44, 45. **Open** 11am-11pm Mon-Wed; 11am-midnight Thur-Sat; 12.30-11pm Sun. **Credit** AmEx, MC, V.

As close as you'll come to a country pub in Edinburgh, the Sheep Heid sits at the foot of Arthur's Seat, near to Duddingston Loch. It's an authentic and aged 'howf'; legend has it that the pub got its name from the motif on a snuff box gifted by James VI of Scotland before he legged it to London to become James I and VI of Great Britain. The food's good, the beer's well kept, and there are few finer venues for a drink and meal if you've tramped over Arthur's Seat at the weekend. Lots of other people know that too, of course.

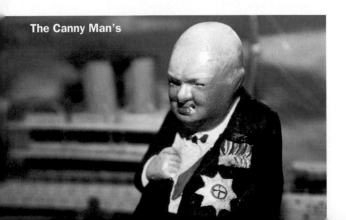

The Canny Man's

Edinburgh: West

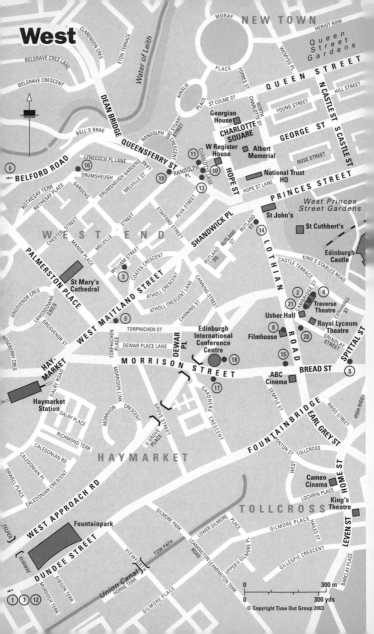

You could say that the areas of Edinburgh covered in this guide, chapter by chapter, have a discrete identity. But West Edinburgh? That's a tougher proposition. Around the west end of Princes Street there are all the eating and drinking options you would expect of a city centre, while the financial services area – the Exchange, based in the triangle formed by Lothian Road, Morrison Street and the West Approach Road – also has a good range of restaurants and watering holes. Lothian Road itself is one of Edinburgh's buzzier streets with nearby theatres, including the Traverse, concert halls and roving bands of young people going from pub to pub on the weekend. Further out, among the tenements of Dalry and Gorgie, good eating and drinking options are rare.

Restaurants

Asian

The Indian Cavalry Club

3 Atholl Place, off West Maitland Street (228 2974). Bus 3, 4, 12, 21, 25, 26, 31, 33, 44. **Meals served** 11am-2.30pm, 5.30pm-midnight daily. **Average** ££. **Credit** AmEx, DC, MC, V.

Waiters in quasi-military costume and set meals with names such as Our Regimental Banquet either appal or appeal. However, if the imperial environment doesn't

Edinburgh: West

bring out the mutineer in you, the Cavalry Club has a lot going for it. The decor is relatively sparse, even attractive, with hanging curtains and plants. There's the usual Indian starters (pakora, kebabs), but also excellent fresh poori with fillings such as lamb, chicken, prawn and various veggie options. There are several set meals for two or more, and an à la carte menu. The latter includes far from clichéd fare such as chilli-fried cod fillet and Kathmandu chicken (barbecued chicken in cinnamon, spring onion and lentil sauce with ginger). Even a staple like tarka dahl is a cut above the norm: a good thick soup-stew that's not swimming in oil. Conversely, the confectionery desserts may be a bit much for some.

Rainbow Arch/
Ho Ho Mei Noodle Shack

8-16A Morrison Street (221 1288). Bus 1, 10, 11, 15, 16, 17, 24, 34. **Meals served** noon-midnight daily. **Average** £. **Credit** AmEx, MC, V.

What you get here very much depends on what you want. The Rainbow Arch has the look and atmosphere of a plush and proper Chinese restaurant (with a friendly welcome from the waitresses, mind you), while the adjacent Noodle Shack is a basic gobble 'n' go affair, open late and more suited to a snack after the pub or between social engagements. The Rainbow Arch's menu has a scope so wide it could be intimidating, with dozens and dozens of choices. There's a decent selection for veggies in terms of starters, soups and mains (27 at last count), while the omnivorous diner could opt for barbecued spare ribs to start, and a simple salted and spicy pork chop as a main, with some bamboo shoots and water chestnuts on the side. It's very 'traditional' in Chinese restaurant terms, but convenient given its position just off Lothian Road. And remember the noodle alternative.

Thai Orchid

44 Grindlay Street (228 4438). Bus 1, 10, 11, 15, 16, 17, 24, 34. **Meals served** noon-2.30pm, 5.30pm-midnight Mon-Fri; 5.30pm-midnight Sat. **Average** ££. **Credit** AmEx, DC, MC, V.

Handy for all kinds of arts venues (the Filmhouse, Usher Hall, Traverse Theatre, Lyceum Theatre), this family-run eaterie has beavered away quietly for some years, taking care with the basic ingredients, and building its reputation. Neither spectacular nor trendy, with a predominantly green decor, it's the kind of place that comes to nestle in your affections. Vegetarians have a good choice, with starters like todd mun kao pode (deep-fried sweetcorn cakes with sweet and sour peanut and coriander dip) and such mains as the all-encompassing kwaitiep pad tow-hu (noodles with tofu, egg and bean-

Mexican restaurant/bar **Cuba Norte** (192 Morrison Street, 221 1430) has a dancefloor downstairs with salsa sounds.

sprouts, all topped with peanuts, chilli and lime). There's a wide range of other dishes, of course, including old reliables such as goong chup peng todd (tempura-style prawns) and gaeng kiew wan (green coconut milk curry with chicken or prawns).

Mediterranean

Lafayette ★
9 Randolph Place (225 8678/www.lafayette.co.uk). Bus 13, 19, 29, 36, 37, 41, 42. **Meals served** noon-2pm, 6.30-10pm Mon-Sat. **Average** £££. **Credit** AmEx, MC, V.
Tudor-style architecture may not turn any heads in the Home Counties, but it's a definite anomaly in Edinburgh; all the more anomalous then to find a French restaurant in such an English building in the Scottish capital. Lafayette is on the first floor; its bright space is defined by wood panelling, yellow paint, a blue carpet and an open fire. Service is very French ('Bon appetit!') and adept, the wine selection is good, and a typical three courses could bring a gorgeous smoked haddock mousse with excellent horseradish vinaigrette to start; Border lamb casserole with marengo sauce as a main; and walnut tart with crème fraîche as a pud. At weekday lunchtimes, Lafayette is popular with the better-heeled variety of men in suits; it's more mixed in the evenings. Easily one of the top five French establishments in the city.

Piatto Verde
7 Dundee Terrace (228 2588). Bus 1, 28, 34, 35. **Meals served** 5-11pm Tue-Thur, Sun; 5pm-midnight Fri, Sat. Closed 2wks Sept. **Average** £. **Credit** MC, V.
People have been falling in love with tiny Piatto Verde ever since it opened in early 1999. Maybe it's the all-muck-in-together nature of the establishment, which feels like a converted tenement living room. There are tables for twos and fours, but drop-in diners may find themselves sharing with others. The menu offers antipasti, salads, breads, pasta, risotto and meat (carne section aside, about 50% is meat- and fish-free, so it's great for vegetarians). Starters such as minestrone soup or baked king prawns are rough and ready, but all the better for it. Seafood risotto is made properly and full of actual seafood, while a vegetarian version (asparagus) is creamy beyond words. With tiramisu, grappa and espresso to finish off, this is a neighbourhood gem.

Pizza Express
32 Queensferry Street (225 8863/www.pizzaexpress.com). Bus 13, 19, 29, 36, 37, 41, 42, Princes Street buses. **Meals served** 11.30am-midnight daily. **Average** £. **Credit** AmEx, DC, MC, V.

Still the no-brainer. You're visiting the city, you've been making consumer choices all day and finally you just want to flop down in a familiar and dependable place and have a pizza – that's what Pizza Express is here for. Yes, it's a chain restaurant, but one of the UK's best. The Queensferry Street branch is a couple of minutes from the west end of Princes Street, bang in the city centre, and you can just about order blind from the menu: say, tuna and cannellini bean salad to start, a glass of Chianti, some Italian sparkling water, then a pizza alle noci (with walnuts, gorgonzola and spinach). The decor is contemporary but familiar.

Branches: 23 North Bridge, Old Town (557 6411); 1 Deanhaugh Street, New Town & Stockbridge (332 7229); 38 The Shore, North-east & Leith (554 4332).

Pompadour ★

Caledonian Hilton Hotel, Princes Street (222 8888). Princes Street buses. **Meals served** 12.30-2.30pm, 7-10pm Tue-Fri; 7-10pm Sat. Closed 2wks Jan. **Average** £££. **Credit** AmEx, DC, MC, V.

This old Edwardian railway hotel houses the most traditionally opulent restaurant in the city. First impressions of the Pompadour leave you scrabbling for

Santini

the right word ('rococo? baroque?'); you browse the menu in an ante-room, then a waiter escorts you to your table, carrying any unfinished G&Ts on a silver tray. The staff glide around soundlessly and if you order something as simple as asparagus with hollandaise as a starter, the accompanying lemon wedge comes wrapped in muslin lest your fingers are sullied by citric detritus. The food is elaborate with roots in haute French cuisine. That means a typical starter being timbale of snow crab with king prawns on watercress sauce, garnished with poached crawfish claw; a main might be cumin-roasted lamb with sweet potato sauté, aubergine confit and spiced pan jus. Crème vanilla with wild berries is one of the simpler – but almost perfect – desserts. Dining tip: dress smart.

Santini/Santini Bis ★

8 Conference Square (221 7788). Bus 1, 10, 11, 15, 16, 17, 22, 24, 34. **Meals served** noon-2.30pm, 6.30-10.30pm Mon-Fri; 6.30-10.30pm Sat. **Average** Santini £££; Santini Bis ££. **Credit** AmEx, DC, MC, V.
Conference Square is right in the middle of Edinburgh's financial district. Scottish Widows is across the way, while the Edinburgh International Conference Centre,

Standard Life and the back of the Sheraton Hotel complete the architectural claustrophobia. In among all this sits Santini; it arrived in 2001 and gathered plaudits before the first char-grilled baby cuttlefish had time to yelp 'Mama!'. There are actually two eateries: the more formal Santini and the adjacent designer-bistro Santini Bis. Both are the antithesis of rubber mozzarella, making excellent use of fresh ingredients. Santini offers wonders such as smoked swordfish carpaccio to start, then vegetarian options, meat and fish. These might entail pumpkin ravioli, scallops with langoustine, beetroot, spring onion and celeriac or grilled baby chicken with a spicy chilli and herb sauce. Ricotta mousse with fig sauce is quite a dessert. Santini Bis is every bit as accomplished. One of the city's very top Italians.

Scalini ★

10 Melville Place (220 2999/www.scaliniristorante.com). *Bus 13, 19, 29, 36, 37, 41, 42.* **Meals served** noon-2pm, 6-10pm Mon-Sat. **Average** ££. **Credit** AmEx, DC, MC, V.

Among the traffic and hassle of the West End, you walk down Scalini's stairs into a small blue basement space

and immediately feel more peaceful. Proprietor Silvio Praino is one of the city's friendlier and more voluble restaurateurs, and he runs an establishment where people really care about food. The antipasti della casa will be brought over and shown to you – it always looks good – while other starters generally involve pasta (ravioli del giorno or linguine al pesto genovese, for example). Mains might include thin-sliced salmon cooked with balsamic vinegar or calf's liver with onion and wine. Desserts are simple: lemon sorbet with vodka or pine nut and custard cake. One of the most exciting features is the wine. There's the 'normal' list – affordable – plus a range of Italians dating from the 1950s (with a 1945 Marchesi de Barolo at £485, if no one's quaffed it all yet).

Modern European

The Atrium ★
10 Cambridge Street (228 8882/www.atriumrestaurant. co.uk). Bus 1, 10, 11, 15, 16, 17, 24, 34. **Meals served** noon-2pm, 6-10.30pm Mon-Fri; 6-10.30pm Sat. **Average** £££. **Credit** AmEx, DC, MC, V.

Rogue.
See p126.

Who's the daddy? One answer in this city. Andrew Radford's flagship restaurant burst on the scene in 1993 and changed the rules of the game as far as top Edinburgh eateries were concerned. Its design still looks contemporary, with low-key lighting, dark wood and copper fixtures and fittings all adding to a real sense of atmosphere and otherness. It's in the same building as the Traverse Theatre (*see p128*) and sister establishment blue bar-café (*see below*). This is destination dining that has stood the test of time. A typical three-course dinner would include the likes of seared scallops and monkfish with belly pork and spicy vinaigrette to start, fillet of sea bass with spinach, fondant potato and aubergine caviar as a main, and traditional custard tart with warm poached blackberries to finish. The wine list is one of the best. Flexible enough to be romantic or businesslike, this is high calibre all round.

Restaurant at the Bonham

35 Drumsheugh Gardens (623 9319/www.thebonham.com). *Princes Street buses.* **Meals served** 12.30-2.30pm, 6.30-10pm daily. **Average** £££. **Credit** AmEx, DC, MC, V.
The Bonham is one of Edinburgh's more designery hotels, discreetly positioned in the West End but only a few minutes' walk from Princes Street. The ground-floor restaurant has a large window admitting lots of light (Scottish weather permitting), and there's a real aspiration to provide excellent service without fuss or servility. Lawyers and financial services types eat at weekday lunchtimes; residents and destination diners in the evenings. A starter as simple as tomato, coconut and lemongrass soup is executed in a manner that makes you sit up and take notice, while a main like fried salmon fillet with confit of fennel and provençale dressing shows that the kitchen pays commendable attention to detail. The menu is creative without going over the top, desserts deft (home-made nougat glacé with mint crème anglaise, for example), the surroundings roomy, the house wines well chosen and the staff most capable.

Rogue ★

Scottish Widows Building, 67 Morrison Street (228 2700/ *www.rogues-uk.com). Bus 1, 10, 11, 15, 16, 17, 22, 24,* *34.* **Meals served** noon-2.30pm, 6-11pm Mon-Sat. **Average** £££. **Credit** AmEx, MC, V.
Rogue burst on to the Edinburgh scene in 2001 to acclaim from all quarters. Proprietor David Ramsden had already established his reputation with (fitz)Henry in Leith (*see p83*) and the high design concepts of Rogue took him to another level. Given its location – firmly in the city's financial district – it's no surprise that its lunchtime clientele is drawn from local offices; evenings are much

The **Golden Rule** (28-30 Yeaman Place, 622 7112), near the UGC cinema complex at Fountain Park, is a decent bar in an unfashionable part of town.

more visually interesting for people-watchers. The menu is informal, offering everything from soups and starters to pizza, pasta, grills, seafood, meat and a few vegetarian options. If you want to sit in spacious, draped surroundings and just have a dish of spaghetti with baby clams and herbs, you can. But a fuller exploration of the menu could bring asparagus with herb vinaigrette and bacon to start, braised veal with fava beans and gnocchi as a main, then a dessert such as coconut panna cotta with lime syrup. Rogue is right up there.

Café-bars & Cafés

blue bar-café ★

10 Cambridge Street (221 1222/www.bluebarcafe.com). Bus 1, 10, 11, 15, 16, 17, 24, 34. **Open** 11.30am-11.45pm Mon-Thur; 11.30am-12.45am Fri, Sat. **Meals served** noon-3pm, 6-10.45pm Mon-Sat. **Average** £. **Credit** AmEx, DC, MC, V.
Don't come here just for a drink; the food puts many local restaurants to shame. Sister establishment to the grander Atrium downstairs (*see p125*), blue offers everything from a pint of lager to a glass of house white with an elaborate sandwich or an accomplished three-course experience in Modern European style. That might be salad of crab, globe artichoke and marjoram oil to start, followed by cumin-crusted tuna and spiced aubergine and ending with some signature Malteser ice-cream. At lunchtime, suits predominate, but in the afternoon and evening the diners are a more mixed lot (the Traverse Theatre is in the same building). Service is peachy keen, the decor modern bordering on stark and the atmosphere relaxed, although the noise levels can get distracting.

Café Newton

Dean Gallery, 72 Belford Road (623 7132). Bus 13. **Open** 10am-4.30pm daily. **Average** £. **No credit cards**.
As gallery cafés go, this may not be Edinburgh's biggest, but it is its grandest. The large windows let light flood in, the fixtures and fittings are all very tasteful (black wood tables and chairs, an ornate silver coffee machine with eagle atop) and the high ceiling underwrites a sense of pomp. Throughout the day you can have tea or coffee with shortbread or lemon and almond polenta cake, but more substantial snacking calls for the lunch menu. This includes soup, specials (leek and brie tart, chicken and mushroom curry) and flavour-packed rosemary focaccia with such fillings as pimento mayonnaise, smoked chicken, roasted peppers and basil. Café Newton has around 30 seats, so if it's full, stroll over the road to the

Scottish National Gallery of Modern Art (75 Belford Road, 624 6200); its café is bigger, has seats outside in summer and serves some fab cheeses.

Filmhouse Bar

88 Lothian Road (229 5932/www.filmhousecinema.com). Bus 1, 10, 11, 15, 16, 17, 24, 34. **Open** 10am-11.30pm Mon-Thur, Sun; 10am-12.30am Fri, Sat. **Meals served** noon-10pm daily. **Average** £. **Credit** MC, V.

The city's main art-house cinema, the Filmhouse has been around for over 20 years, but the bar was refurbished in 2002 so it doesn't look as dowdy as you'd think. It's the ideal place to meet friends before or after a movie, but also for snacks, light meals and drinks. The draught beer is pretty respectable (cask ales including the locally brewed and organic Golden Promise) and there's an industrious kitchen making pizzas, light curries, soup and salads. Customers include everyone from serious-looking film students discussing Fellini over a lingering latte to bands of drinkers in for the movie quiz.

Indigo Yard

7 Charlotte Lane (220 5603/www.indigoyardedinburgh. co.uk). Bus 13, 19, 29, 36, 37, 41, 42. **Open** 8.30am-1am daily. **Meals served** 8.30am-10pm daily. **Average** ££. **Credit** AmEx, MC, V.

Indigo Yard made quite a splash when it descended on the West End in the mid '90s, with its high design values (canvas canopies, exposed brickwork, a balcony level), aspirational menus and service. These days it has found a niche catering to a fairly mature but up-for-it crowd on weekend evenings, while classic Edinburgh businesses are the bulk clientele at lunch and after work. That means middle-aged male suits as well as groups of female customer service reps necking Bacardi Breezers. (But tastefully.) You can stop in just for coffee, but there's also breakfast (french toast with bacon and maple syrup) and sandwiches (hot mozzarella and parma ham), as well as main meals (griddled cod with salsa verde, wild mushroom risotto, charred ribeye steak). Some people come for a sit-down three-course dinner; many others for a snack, a raspberry Martini or a bottle or three of semillon chardonnay.

Traverse Theatre Bar

Traverse Theatre, 10 Cambridge Street (228 5383/ www.virtualtraverse.com). Bus 1, 10, 11, 15, 16, 17, 24, 34. **Open** 10am-midnight Mon-Wed; 10.30am-1am Thur-Sat; 5pm-midnight Sun. **Meals served** noon-8pm daily. **Average** £. **Credit** MC, V.

One of the main venues for the city's international arts festival every August, with two theatre spaces, the Trav gets very busy pre- and post-performance all year round.

Edinburgh: West

Traverse Theatre Bar

It's a modern, roomy venue with an inside-out ceiling (ducts and conduits as a design feature) that attracts a typical café-bar crowd. Food specials might include king prawn and smoked haddock chowder or lamb and spinach curry. The snackier regular menu features ciabatta sandwiches, potato wedges and bacon baguettes in the morning and a nachos 'n' lager special offer in the evening. There's always a single malt whisky (Ardbeg, Glenmorangie) and decent bottled beer, plus Leffe and Hoegaarden on tap. It's in the same building as blue (*see p127*) and the Atrium (*see p125*).

Pubs & Bars

The Athletic Arms

1-3 Angle Park Terrace (337 3822). Bus 1, 28, 34, 35.
Open 11am-midnight Mon-Thur; 11am-1am Fri, Sat; 12.30-11pm Sun. **No credit cards.**

The **Roseburn Bar** (located at 1 Roseburn Terrace, 337 1067) is near Murrayfield and always packed before international rugby games.

Before the 1980s – archaeological in eating and drinking terms – Edinburgh wasn't exactly blessed with a surfeit of style bars or decent real ale pubs. But there were a few places around the city with a reputation for one reason or another, such as the grand Café Royal, for example (*see p70*), and the late-Victorian Athletic Arms. Everyone called it Diggers, and they still do (gravediggers used to come here; Dalry Cemetery is across the street), but its fame was based on the fact that it was said to serve the

Ale and hearty

Scottish beer is generally richer, heavier and maltier than English beer, as it uses fewer hops. It's often referred to in terms of shillings (written /-), usually prefaced by 70 or 80. The derivation of such odd terminology is unclear, but one theory suggests that shillings originally denoted the cost of the barrel of beer. The number of shillings certainly gives an indication of the strength of the beer, with 80/- (often known as 'export' because it was sent out to soldiers in India) stronger than 70/- (also called 'heavy').

Two enormous industrial plants dominate the Scottish brewing industry: **Tennent Caledonian**'s Wellpark Brewery in Glasgow and **Scottish Courage**'s Fountainbridge Brewery in Edinburgh. Between them they produce the bulk of the beer sold across the country: iconic drinks like Tennent's Lager and Tennent's

Special (Tennent Caledonian); and McEwan's 70/-, McEwan's 80/- and McEwan's Lager (Scottish Courage). Virtually every bar in Scotland will stock one or more of these; they have big marketing departments to keep their profiles high; and if you were creating an ark with representative artefacts of Scottish culture, the popularity of these brews would ensure that at least a couple were included.

Scottish Courage is a huge concern with seven breweries across the UK and Ireland, so whether you're drinking McEwan's 80/- in Edinburgh, Beamish Stout in Cork or Newcastle Brown in Newcastle-upon-Tyne, you're drinking the products of the same group. Tennent Caledonian, meanwhile, is now a subsidiary of the Belgian company Interbrew, the second largest brewer in the world.

Consolidation in the industry has been going on for a long time. Take Edinburgh: towards the end of the 19th century it had something like 40 breweries and a worldwide reputation for the quality of 'Edinburgh ales' that had built up over hundreds of years. Monks at Holyrood Abbey were making beer as early as the 12th century and by the 16th there was enough commercial brewing to justify the formation of a Society of Brewers.

The celebrity and viability of Edinburgh ales peaked along with the British Empire, but after World War II a falling off in colonial markets meant the city's breweries were stagnating and susceptible to takeover. By the 1990s there were only two in operation, both in the west: the big one at Fountainbridge, and the artisan Caledonian Brewery on Slateford Road, home of cask ales Caledonian 80/- and Deuchars IPA.

If this sounds like a sad tale of decline, it's not. At the megacorp end of the market, Scottish Courage and Tennent Caledonian may be well-established fixtures, but since the 1970s the sheer ubiquity of mass-produced beer has created its own antithesis. The real ale revival since then has seen smaller specialist concerns spring up all over the Scotland, just as they have in England. The **Broughton Brewery** near Biggar, around 30 miles south of Edinburgh, was among the first, back in 1979. **Harviestoun Brewery** in Dollar, near Stirling, arrived in 1984; the **Orkney Brewery** at Stromness in 1988; the **Tomintoul Brewery** in the Highlands east of Aberdeen in 1993; and even one on the Isle of Arran (the **Arran Brewery**, of course) as recently as 2000.

Currently the number of small breweries – including microbreweries attached to pubs – is around two dozen. Beers vary from the rich, malty **Dark Island** (Orkney) to award-winning, cask-conditioned lager such as **Schiehallion** (Harviestoun). Good pubs across Edinburgh and Glasgow will have at least some such beers available on tap; specialist off-licences and even a number of supermarkets have bottled versions of the more popular brands.

Meanwhile, **Heather Ale** of Strathhaven, Lanarkshire, actually makes beers based on Scottish recipes dating back to the Dark Ages, but adapted to modern expectations – so no floaty bits. **Fraoch** is made with heather flowers (the Picts were said to drink a heather ale), **Alba** uses pine sprigs and spruce shoots (an idea introduced by the Vikings), while **Grozet** is a gooseberry beer that was around in the 16th century and probably before. Scotland may be awash with Tennent's Lager and McEwan's 80/-, but it's worth remembering that there is an alternative.

best pint of McEwan's 80/- in the city, brewed less than half a mile away at the huge Fountainbridge Brewery. Generations of students loved it for its good beer and working class vérité, while to the locals it was just 'their local'. Nowadays, the 80/- is still well cared for; it's a basic, tidy, old-fashioned 'howf' (formica tables, leather seats), and worth checking out just to see what good pubs were like when your dad was a lad.

Bert's

29-31 William Street (225 5748). Bus 3, 4, 12, 21, 25, 26, 31, 33. **Open** 11am-11pm Mon-Wed; 11am-midnight Thur-Sat. **Credit** AmEx, MC, V.

Bert's looks like a traditional old pub, but it's not; it was just designed that way. Artifice aside, it still serves good beer, great pies, filled ciabattas and, for anyone who has been through the hell that is Princes Street on a Saturday afternoon, it offers blessed and handy sanctuary. The decor is all dark wood and green leather seats, and draught beers include Caledonian 80/-, Deuchars IPA and others (Marston's Pedigree, perhaps). It can be a bit of a rugby lovers' haunt, so be prepared for a crowded house when Scotland are playing at Murrayfield.

Branch: 2-4 Raeburn Place, New Town & Stockbridge (332 6345).

Blue Blazer

2 Spittal Street (229 5030). Bus 2, 35. **Open** 11am-1am daily. **Credit** MC, V.

Caught between the bustle of Lothian Road and the hustle of nearby lap dancing bars (Edinburgh's 'pubic triangle'), the Blue Blazer is a haven of sanity in the shadow of the Castle. There's nothing stylish or pretentious about this pub: it just has two small rooms where punters can sit and sip decent whisky or try one of (usually) eight cask ales (Marston's Pedigree or Caledonian 80/-, for example). Where chain pubs have come and gone, the Blue Blazer has carved a niche and survived; long may it continue.

Caley Sample Room

58 Angle Park Terrace (337 7204). Bus 4, 28, 35. **Open** 11am-midnight Mon-Thur, Sun; 11am-1am Fri, Sat. **Credit** AmEx, MC, V.

The Caley is red brick on the outside, roomy on the inside, with wooden benches in the middle of the room and a simple, functional decor. And it's just a few minutes' walk from the Caledonian Brewery on Slateford Road, so a good place to sample the Caledonian 80/- and Deuchars IPA brewed there. Other ales are available too, and basic bar food. Given its proximity to Tynecastle (Heart of Midlothian FC's ground), it gets packed before and after games. Murrayfield is nearby too, so the same goes for when Scotland is playing (rugby union) at home.

Fancy a pint while waiting for a train at Haymarket Station? Try **Ryrie's Bar** (Haymarket Terrace, 337 7582), which dates back to 1862.

Where to...

Glasgow:
City centre

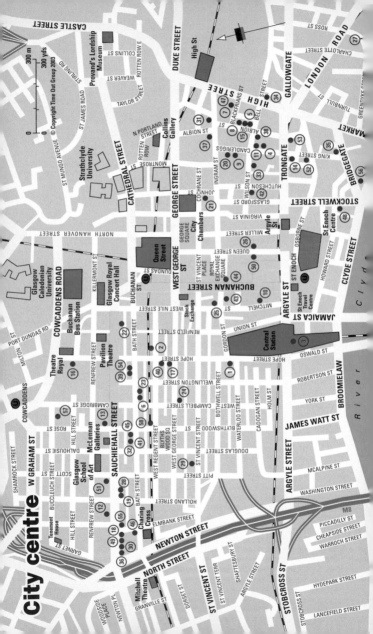

MAP KEY

The centre of Glasgow is certainly not as visually spectacular as the centre of Edinburgh, and lacks the capital's historic if sometimes quaint charm – but it does have its own appeal. Anyone still harbouring creaky notions about it being a rough or unsafe city should relax – although the council can go a bit overboard in proclaiming Glasgow a cosmopolitan European metropolis. The main nightlife areas are around Buchanan Street, Sauchiehall Street and the newly gentrified Merchant City, although efforts are being made to liven up the riverfront area at the Clyde too. The centre is a reasonable size – you can walk through it in under an hour, or jump on the circular Underground line. There's a rapid turnover of the latest eating places and style bars, as well as traditional drinking haunts. The idea of deep-fried Mars bars is mostly a joke, but the city centre is well served by takeaways too.

Glasgow: City centre

Restaurants

Asian

Amber Regent

50 West Regent Street (331 1655). Buchanan Street underground. **Meals served** noon-2.25pm, 5.30-11.30pm Mon-Thur; noon-midnight Sat. **Average £££. Credit** AmEx, DC, MC, V.

The Amber Regent enjoys a reputation as one of Glasgow's finest Chinese restaurants. In some respects, the cuisine is not so vastly superior to its rivals, but the luxurious, rather old-fashioned surroundings and the little touches, such as the brass spoon rests, are a badge of its class. The expansive menu offers some refreshingly original choices at higher than average prices (starters £5 or £6, mains around £15). The seafood selection is prodigious, with king prawns available in every conceivable incarnation. Other tempting dishes include chicken in garlic and plum sauce, and grilled fillet steak Chinese style (with honey and wine sauce). Service is highly attentive if a little brisk. And there is certainly one

Ichiban. *See p140.*

area in which the Amber Regent conforms to average Chinese restaurant standards – the terrible background muzak of MOR hits.

Canton Express

407 Sauchiehall Street (332 0145). Charing Cross rail.
Meals served noon-midnight daily. **Average** £.
No credit cards.

This Cantonese fast-food joint is a legend with drinkers and clubbers at the Charing Cross end of Sauchiehall Street, thanks to its conducive late-night opening hours and terrific value. Ideally situated to catch revellers from the Garage and the Art School students' union, as well as its many patrons from Glasgow's Chinatown area in Garnethill, the Canton is a rough-and-ready place with a certain charm to its ultra-bright neon strip lighting, formica table tops, open kitchen and treacherous (for the inebriated) journey down the back stairs to the toilet. The food is basic, certainly fast, generously portioned, sometimes dubiously coloured and loaded with mono-sodium glutamate – but it hits on the tastebuds, and should be washed down with a big pot of Chinese tea. The Canton enjoys a steady trade through the day, then comes alive as other places are winding down.

China Buffet King

345-349 Sauchiehall Street (333 1788/1799). Charing Cross rail. **Meals served** 11.45am-11pm daily. **Average** £. **Credit** MC, V.

Roll up, roll up for this new enterprise, and then roll out after eating all you can for the meagre sum of £9.99 (weekend), £8.99 (weekdays) or £6.99 (Sun) – it's even cheaper at lunch (weekdays £5.80) and during early evening 'happy hour' (£6.80). Glaswegians love a bargain as much as they love their oriental food, and the China Buffet King has queues out of the door at peak times (they don't take advance bookings) and is nearly always a blur of noise and activity. The wonder is that no one thought of such a simple idea in Glasgow earlier: give your guests a plate and let them loose on a hot and cold buffet comprising sure-fire Chinese faves, such as chow meins, foo yung and sweet and sour dishes. The food, like the dining hall decor, is neither fancy nor adventurous, but it's certainly tasty. Staff bring your drinks to the table, but the rest of the service is up to you, so prepare for traffic jams at the food stations. Already a favourite with families (curiously, children under 4.5ft tall eat for £3.80) and for celebrations.

Ichiban ★

50 Queen Street (204 4200/www.ichiban.co.uk). St Enoch underground/Queen Street rail. **Meals served** noon-10pm Mon-Wed; noon-11pm Thur-Sat; 1-10pm Sun. **Average** £. **Credit** AmEx, DC, MC, V.

Translating as 'number one', Ichiban could be making its own quietly confident statement about its position in Glasgow's Japanese restaurant stakes – and it would not get much argument from its mixed clientele, who willingly queue for a seat at one of the communal canteen tables. The Japanese love order and the procedure at Ichiban is thus: salivate over the menu and make your choice from the starters (including sushi, wun tuns and tempura) and the ramen and udon noodle main courses, whether pan-fried or in a soup. Your waiter taps the order into a little electronic pad, writes the corresponding dish number on your paper tablemat and, before you've had time to swig a drop of Asahi, your meal arrives direct from the open kitchen for your delectation. Don't forget some heated saki to make the experience go with a zing. Not the place for an intimate, romantic meal, but it is the destination of choice for bustle, quality and incredibly good value. The West End branch is slightly larger. **Branch**: 184 Dumbarton Road, West End (334 9222).

Kama Sutra

331 Sauchiehall Street (332 0055/www.kama-sutra-restaurant.com). Charing Cross rail. **Meals served** noon-midnight Mon-Sat; 5pm-midnight Sun. **Average** £. **Credit** AmEx, DC, MC, V.

Gourmet deli/off-licence **Peckham's** (www.peckhams.co.uk) has branches in both Glasgow and Edinburgh. The largest covers four floors at 61-65 Glassford Street (553 0666) in the Merchant City.

Glasgow: City centre

Kama Sutra

With menu headings such as Old Flames, Saucy Suggestions and Present Day Pleasures, this spicy Indian restaurant wears its lurve theme on its sleeve. When Kama Sutra opened, it was Glasgow's first attempt at a stylish curry house and, almost a decade later, the attraction is still strong. Paradoxically, it is not really an ideal choice for an intimate dinner date *à deux*, as its popularity pulls in larger parties to revel in the sumptuous dishes and decor – all wrought-iron detail and rich drapes rather than the trad flock wallpaper and quaint murals. Curry lovers have an alluring array of options: pakoras, bhajis and dosas to start, followed by meat, fish or vegetable bhunas, dopiazas, baltis, biryanis, all rated according to their spiciness. The more adventurous can opt for a butter masala or malaidar (chilli, garlic and spinach) creation, something from the tandoori section or a thali (for two or four people) with a variety of dishes for £15.95 per person.

Loon Fung

417-419 Sauchiehall Street (332 1240). Charing Cross rail. **Meals served** noon-11.30pm daily. **Average** ££. **Credit** AmEx, DC, MC, V.

Avid patronage by the Chinese community is generally the sign of a good oriental restaurant, and Loon Fung does not disappoint. You get the full Cantonese experience here: waiters in brocade waistcoats escort you past the exotic fish tank into an open-plan room decorated with dragon frescoes and paper lanterns, to tables set with willow pattern crockery, while ambient Chinese music ripples in the background. The only element missing is a game of mah-jong in a back room. The food is every bit as authentic. Start with something from the wide range of dim sum – scallop dumplings or oyster beancurd, say – and follow with monkfish hotpot or baked oysters with roast pork belly. There's also a generous choice of beef, pork and chicken dishes and a lesser but adequate vegetarian selection. Desserts are the routine ice-cream concoctions, as depicted on a separate laminated menu. The two-course business lunch is a bargain at £5.95.

Mao ★

84 Brunswick Street (564 5161/www.cafemao.com).
St Enoch underground/Argyle Street rail. **Meals served** noon-11pm Mon-Thur; noon-11.30pm Fri, Sat; 1-10pm Sun. **Average** ££. **Credit** AmEx, MC, V.
Mao is a great example of clued-up Glaswegian dining, as proved by the fact that its two floors are frequently packed. The food is a hip, imaginative mish-mash of Chinese, Japanese and South-east Asian cooking, while the decor – primary coloured furniture and Warholian

Mao

prints of Mao on the walls – is as vibrant as some of the truly lip-smacking flavours. Munch on a side order of shrimp crackers to get the tastebuds up and running, or pick from unusual starter options, such as chilli squid, tempura tofu or duck and lychee salad. Main courses include penang duck curry, stir-fried tiger prawn with hokkien noodles, and nasi goreng. Portions are hefty; if you do manage to hit the bottom of your noodle bowl, you can plug any remaining gap with white chocolate cheesecake or a selection of sorbets. Service is chirpy to match the zing of the food.

OKO

68 Ingram Street (572 1500/www.okorestaurants.com). St Enoch underground/Queen Street rail. **Meals served** noon-3pm, 6-11pm Tue-Thur; noon-3pm, 6pm-midnight Fri; noon-midnight Sat; 5.30-10.30pm Sun. **Average** £. **Credit** AmEx, MC, V.

Simple Minds' main man Jim Kerr has left behind his white leather blousons and black eyeliner and invested his talents and finances in this super-chic sushi restaurant. Occupying the ground floor of the eminently desirable Todd Building, its minimalist interior (designed by local trendy architects ZOO) in bare stone, natural wood and stainless steel is suitably zen, raising OKO a notch above the homogeneous look of chains such as Yo! Sushi. You still get the sushi dining staple of a conveyor belt from which to pluck your nigiri, sashimi and maki. If you don't see what you want, ask for it. Hot dishes such as chicken yakitori can be ordered separately. As with any sushi restaurant, the bill can mount up as inexorably as the colour-coded plates, but the Sunday night buffet – a choice of more than 40 dishes for £15 – is a top deal. The delightful mezzanine bar, OKO-hi, is underused; its only drawback is a tendency to use Simple Minds' greatest hits as background music.

Peking Inn

191 Hope Street (332 7120). Buchanan Street underground/Central Station rail. **Meals served** noon-2pm, 5.30-11pm Mon-Thur; noon-2pm, 5.30pm-midnight Fri, Sat; 5.30-11pm Sun. **Average** ££. **Credit** AmEx, DC, MC, V.

With its fresh, simple, green and white decor, the Peking Inn is an unassuming Chinese restaurant that keeps all its flourishes for the cooking. The menu is a whopper, with substantial subsections for soups and the mandatory beef, chicken, duck and king prawn main dishes. But fans of scallops, squid and tofu also have ample choice. Splash out on a whole Peking aromatic duck for £30 or stick to the two-course pre-theatre (£7.95) or business lunch (£6.50); both offer practically the run of the menu, and include a separate vegetarian menu that

is longer than many restaurants' entire veggie provision. To add to the flexibility, almost every dish is available in a smaller portion, so you can eat like a bird or pig out on more than one choice. There are also several sharing banquets including a year of the goat special which offers 'golden rooster' and 'double happiness roast' among other esoteric attractions.

The Wee Curry Shop

7 Buccleuch Street (353 0777). Cowcaddens underground.
Meals served noon-2.30pm, 5.30-10.30pm Mon-Sat.
Average £. No credit cards.
From the people who brought you Mother India (*see p182*), this hidden gem does exactly what it says on the label. A snug (as in sardines), no-frills Indian restaurant tucked a few blocks to the north of Sauchiehall Street's busiest shopping stretch, it enjoys great word of mouth for its simple, flavoursome home cooking. Unlike many of its curry cousins, this dinky establishment doesn't overpower you with an overlong menu; it's pakora or poori to start, while the mains are dominated by chicken dishes and some classic veggie choices, all prepared in the open kitchen. The two-course lunch for £4.75 represents almost indecent value for money. Bring your own bottle and some balti-loving chums – but don't forget to book in advance, as there's only room for 22 curry buffs at any one time.

OKO. *See p143.*

Fish & seafood

Gamba ★
225A West George Street (572 0899). Buchanan Street underground/Central Station rail. **Meals served** noon-2.30pm, 5-10.30pm Mon-Sat. **Average £££. Credit** AmEx, MC, V.

If you think that all that Glaswegians know what to do with fish is dunk it in batter and serve it with chips, try Gamba. They know their fish, from the most basic grilled lemon sole in butter or cod fillet with mushy minted peas, to more adventurous dishes such as tuna sashimi. Most importantly, they emphasise freshly caught fish – and you can certainly taste the difference. Though it's picked up several restaurant-of-the-year awards, Gamba is still not too self-conscious about its success; from the moment you enter the warm, clean-lined interior, you feel comfortable rather than intimidated. Of course, if you don't feel in the mood for fish, it's hardly the best choice, but given their inventive menu, perhaps you could be persuaded? Booking advisable.

Rogano ★
11 Exchange Place, off Buchanan Street (248 4055). Buchanan Street or St Enoch underground. **Meals served** noon-2.30pm, 6.30-10.30pm daily. **Average £££. Credit** AmEx, DC, MC, V.

The fabulous art deco dining room at Rogano, one of the city's most enduring restaurants, recalls the Clyde-built Cunard liners. When John Byrne shot his 1989 TV series *Your Cheatin' Heart* here, the great and the good of Glasgow were a permanent fixture over champagne and oysters. These days, Rogano's star has begun to fade a little as newer, slightly less stuffy restaurants have taken the limelight and its once-legendary fish menu seems to have become fairly passé in a city now swimming in decent cullen skinks. Still, faded glamour has a certain curiosity value, and Rogano remains a highly respectable venue for an important meal (booking is advisable). Staff are discreetly, efficiently excellent.

Mediterranean

Dino's

39 Sauchiehall Street (332 0626). Buchanan Street underground. **Meals served** 7-11pm daily. **Average** £. **Credit** AmEx, DC, MC, V.

A lot of people just love Dino's. About as far as you can get from cheesy mock-Italian chains and as close as you can come to a real taste of ordinary Italy in Scotland, this is a real neighbourhood joint despite its location slap-bang in the middle of town. The food is not, perhaps, gourmet standard (though the thin pizzas are crispy and tasty, and the chicken in red wine is eminently satisfying), but it's good solid stuff. What makes Dino's special is the atmosphere and the charming service; the good wine list doesn't hurt either. The decor is simple and hasn't changed for donkey's years: pictures of Italy, wooden fittings, candles, wine racks. As well as the main restaurant, there are booths in the adjoining wing, where you can get a more basic, café-style menu. And there's a counter selling the most delicious, doughy, stodgy doughnuts. Homer Simpson would approve.

Fratelli Sarti ★

121 Bath Street (204 0440). Buchanan Street underground. **Meals served** 8.30am-10.30pm daily. **Average** £. **Credit** AmEx, MC, V.

There are Italian restaurants and there is Sarti's: a Glasgow institution. It all began with the cosy little café-cum-deli on Wellington Street, though for a more extensive choice and more room, the adjoining Bath Street restaurant is probably a better choice for dinner. In keeping with its unpretentious, simple Italian style – no clichéd tat, just mounds of authentic imported foodstuffs and drinks – just about anyone and everyone eats here. The staff are the real thing too and graciously helpful, whether you're rushing with limited time or need advice on the wine list. The house speciality is the pizza.

Conran's **Zinc Bar & Grill** is due to open at Princes Square, 48 Buchanan Street, at the end of June 2003. The site will also include a more formal French restaurant. Call 0207 716 7811 for more info.

The best cocktails

Candy Bar
Champagne cocktails served in pitchers for a decadent start to a girls' night out. *See p171.*

Lowdown
Sip a vodka Martini or a Mai Tai while nibbling on tapas in this late-opening basement. *See p164.*

Nice'n'Sleazy
Probably the only place on the planet offering cocktails made with Buckfast, a lethal tonic wine of local infamy. *See p175.*

OKO-hi
Occupying the mezzanine of stylish sushi restaurant OKO, this bar is small but perfectly formed – just like its cocktail menu. *See p143.*

Rogano
Meticulously prepared classics – at second-mortgage prices. *See p145.*

Saint Jude's
Live the *Sex and the City* fantasy with a zingy Cosmopolitan in the sleek basement bar. *See p151.*

It's nothing like the doughy supermarket variety: thin, crusty, flavoursome and with an inventive range of fresh toppings (wild boar, anyone?) – filling and yet not stodgy. The seafood and coffees are also good.

Sannino's Pizzeria
61 Bath Street (332 8025). Buchanan Street underground. **Meals served** noon-10.30pm Mon-Wed, Sun; noon-midnight Thur-Sat. **Average** £. **Credit** AmEx, DC, MC, V. Two nearby branches of a superior pizza 'chain', which have the same menu and more or less the same lively, friendly, family-type atmosphere (although Bath Street overlooks the road, whereas the Elmbank branch is in a basement). Prices are decent and so is the menu, if a bit basic. But then, if it's a really good pizza you're after – thin, crunchy and richly topped – why bother scanning a huge list of fripperies? The pasta, breads and wine are good quality too. The decor is similarly unpretentious, with lots of authentic Italian touches.
Branch: 61 Elmbank Street, City centre (332 3565).

Glasgow: City centre

Rogano.
See p145.

Mexican & Cuban

Cuba Norte

17 John Street (552 3505). Queen Street rail/Buchanan Street underground. **Meals served** noon-11pm Mon-Thur; noon-10.30pm Fri-Sun. **Average ££. Credit** AmEx, MC, V.

In a crazy cross-cultural twist, this Latino restaurant is housed alongside the designer stores in the hyper-cool Italian Centre. Inside, though, it's all about Cuba, with traditional music and a bodega-style decor (marble, leafy and natural) complementing the menu of dishes drawn from the country and the Caribbean region. You may, or may not, be surprised to learn that this includes tapas: all the usual Spanish-style ones, plus a few real novelties. The rest of the menu is an intriguing combination of familiar and unusual tastes of meat and fruit, and there's a good veggie selection. The venue holds infectious regular Latin events, including tango and salsa classes and DJs. Needless to say, you can get a Havana cigar too if you want to indulge your Hemingway fantasies.

Pancho Villas

26 Bell Street (552 7737). Queen Street rail/St Enoch underground. **Meals served** noon-10pm Mon-Sat; 6-10pm Sun. **Average £. Credit** AmEx, MC, V.

Mexican restaurants can sometimes seem a bit… well, samey. Many of the dishes are basically variations on the same theme: extra peppers here, refried beans there, a tortilla instead of a taco. But who cares when it's all so sizzlingly spicy and tasty? Though most of us don't know our Mayan from our Tex-Mex, Pancho's is the work of actual Mexican Maira Nunez, who does. As one of the longest-established Mexican restaurants in Glasgow it has certainly introduced many people to the joys of the region by virtue of presenting simple dishes well. Best of all are probably the fajitas (both meat and veggie), which are notable as much for quantity as quality: don't even bother with a starter unless you've been starved for a week. The decor is fun, with lots of bright colours, kitchsy art and statuary; just the job for a cheery night out with a couple of friends and a couple of Margaritas.

Modern European

Arthouse Grill ★

129 Bath Street (572 6002/www.arthousehotel.com).
Buchanan Street underground. **Meals served** 7-10.30am, noon-3pm, 5-10.30pm daily. **Average** ££. **Credit** AmEx, DC, MC, V.
The Arthouse is one of Glasgow's hip hotels, ideally located to capitalise on the burgeoning dining/drinking scene along Bath Street. But its own basement restaurant is easily the equal of its neighbours, and gives non-guests the opportunity to wallow in the hotel's classy, ultra-modern interior and goggle at the waterfall feature that sluices down the middle of the main stairwell (take a look en route to the loo). Although the name might suggest a meatfest, it's actually seafood at which the Grill excels, offering tantalising starters such as smoked salmon, lobster and asparagus terrine and mains that include shellfish linguine and pan-fried red snapper with pine nut coulis. There are also numerous vegetarian options. Eminently suitable for entertaining friends, partners or business associates, the Arthouse offers aspirational dining at affordable prices and in congenial surroundings. The compact bar at one end of the restaurant is a dinky place for drinks while you wait for your table.

Loop Restaurant

64 Ingram Street (572 1472). Queen Street rail/St Enoch underground. **Meals served** noon-10pm Tue-Thur; noon-10.30pm Fri, Sat; noon-9pm Sun. **Average** ££. **Credit** AmEx, DC, MC, V.
A modern and funky establishment, Loop seems slightly out of place in staid Ingram Street. Brightly lit, it has a stylish, steely main area on a raised platform and more cosy armchair tables near the door. The informal menu (you don't have a starter, main course and dessert; instead there's 'to begin', 'the middle bit' and 'puddings') has an international air, with samplings of Asian fusion

For a distinctly Scottish sweet treat, try something from the **Tunnocks** range, available almost everywhere. Recommended: the gooey, chocolate-coated teacakes and chewy caramel logs and wafers.

and Thai dishes, as well as more standard fare like chicken, fish, pasta and steaks. Sticky toffee pudding is indeed a gloriously sticky and moist highlight. While Loop has an upmarket feel, it's to be commended for offering bargain starters and light meals for those with shallower pockets, so it also appeals to students at nearby Strathclyde University.

Branch: **Bewley's Hotel** 110 Bath Street, City centre (354 7705).

Papingo

104 Bath Street (332 6678/www.papingo.co.uk).
Buchanan Street underground. **Meals served** noon-2.30pm, 5-10.30pm Mon-Sat; 5-10pm Sun. **Average** ££.
Credit AmEx, MC, V.

The name means parrot (and some subtle parrot motifs appear amid its cosy, intimate decor), though that doesn't give you much of a clue to the nature of this smart basement restaurant. It caters mainly to older couples and business types, who appreciate its slightly formal air. The oft-changing menu features fine Scottish produce like venison and Angus beef, often with an exotic twist in the dressing or spicing. Typical dishes include fish soup with mussels, prawns and lemongrass (starter) and roast lamb and braised fennel with redcurrant and tarragon jus (main). The service and wine list are good, if unimaginative. Papingo is owned by Alan Tomkins, who's also behind Gamba (*see p145*) and Frango (Italian Centre, 15 John Street, 552 4433) – he's clearly fond of those mysterious one-word names – as well as a couple of city bars; he's also current chair of the Glasgow Restaurateurs Association.

Fratelli Sarti.
See p146.

Quigley's

158-166 Bath Street (331 4060). Buchanan Street underground. **Meals served** noon-3pm, 5pm-midnight Mon-Sat. **Average** £££. **Credit** AmEx, MC, V.

One of the more recent additions to the plethora of eateries on Bath Street, and probably the one that Glaswegians would most like to see succeed, as it signals the fulfilment of a 20-year dream for local celebrity chef John Quigley. He's come a long way since cooking for Bryan Adams' on-the-road entourage. Unlike his former employer, Quigley has certainly hit the style pulse, restoring this former auction house to its original Victorian grandeur, while adding a contrasting kick of monochromatic minimalism in the wooden floors, mirrored walls and sleek banquette seating. The food reflects this unorthodox alliance of styles; traditional organic burgers sit side by side with contemporary Pacific Rim-style dishes. The menu changes frequently, and the chef clearly revels in inventive combos. Quigley's is not at its most atmospheric when thinly booked, but general word of mouth, as well as hopes for the place, remain strong.

Saint Jude's

190 Bath Street (352 8800/www.saintjudes.com). Buchanan Street underground. **Meals served** noon-3pm, 6-10.30pm Mon-Thur; noon-3pm, 6-11pm Fri; 6-11pm Sat; 6-10.30pm Sun. **Average** £££. **Credit** AmEx, DC, MC, V.

Another chic Bath Street eaterie, offering much the same pan-global cuisine as Quigley's (*see above*) and the Arthouse Grill (*see p149*) in refined, minimalist surroundings, but with slightly less choice: the seasonal menu typically offers three options per course. Saint

Glasgow: City centre

Jude's is also a boutique hotel, with five bedrooms (if you really can't heave yourself far after partaking of the hospitality) and – arguably its main attraction – a basement bar with a super-stylish but unimposing decor and a backroom lounge that resembles a set from *2001*. It's popular with the Art School set, who hoover up under-£6 lunch options such as beefburger on focaccia and asparagus tortellini. The drinks aren't especially cheap, but watch the pretty things converge when cocktail happy hour arrives.

Tempus@CCA

Centre for Contemporary Arts, 350 Sauchiehall Street (332 7959). Cowcaddens underground/Charing Cross rail. **Open** 11am-11pm Mon-Sat; 11am-6pm Sun. **Meals served** noon-9.30pm Mon-Sat; noon-4pm Sun. **Average** ££. **Credit** AmEx, DC, MC, V.

Glasgow's arts venues don't tend to house especially memorable restaurants, but Tempus is a notable exception, largely due to its impressive setting in the vertiginous atrium of the coolly reinvented Centre for Contemporary Arts. The restaurant, though it may not exemplify intimate dining, has merit. Sleek wooden tables and cream banquettes are laid out with symmetrical precision, and the very reasonably priced menu reflects the exacting standards of the polished modernist architecture. The food can take a while to arrive, but is tasty, offering an imaginative slant on the fail-safe checklist of game/fowl/fish/veg/snacks. Options include beetroot risotto or Thai beef salad (starters), baked hake with mussel and veg cassoulet (main) and apple crumble crème brûlée (pud). Tempus is principally patronised by conceptual art fans, Sauchiehall Street shoppers and all-round hipsters – but don't be surprised if you happen to stumble into a private business function.

The Tron

63 Trongate (552 8587/www.tron.co.uk). St Enoch underground. **Meals served** 10am-8pm Mon-Wed; 10am-11pm Thur-Sat; noon-10pm Sun. **Average** ££. **Credit** AmEx, DC, MC, V.

The Tron is one of Glasgow's most interesting theatres, but its restaurant is far too good to be used just as a place to pop into before a show. It's a venue of two halves: you enter through a modish bar, glass-fronted and filled with the hip and arty perching on funky furniture. Then, at the back, there's a smashing traditional restaurant, all cosy wood and wide tables, with pleasingly stern walls and an old-fashioned bar. The Mod Euro-style food is both good and reasonably priced, focusing on popular dishes like chicken and fish in good-sized portions. The atmosphere is informal, but not too raucous. You might even run into a star there, grabbing a bite before curtain-up.

Tempus@CCA

Scottish

Arisaig ★

24 Candleriggs (552 4251). Argyle Street rail. **Meals served** noon-11pm daily. **Average** ££. **Credit** MC, V.
Until fairly recently, these premises were the city centre branch of Oblomov (*see p196*), which didn't make much of a dent – so let's hope Arisaig's mellow environment and scrummy food prove a recipe for success. The new owners have switched from eastern European to modern Scottish cuisine, but kept the refined interior of rich dark wood. A long, elegantly curved bar leads to the dining area with its well-judged muted lighting. The seasonal menu is not extensive – no more than half a dozen choices per course – but some creativity has been exercised in the combination of flavours across the game and seafood dishes. Unusually for a Scottish restaurant, vegetarians are imaginatively catered for; nettle cakes and lavender loaf might sound like rabbit food, but are as satisfying as the filling potato mashes that accompany most dishes. Service is pleasingly unobtrusive.

Café Gandolfi

Café Gandolfi ★

64 Albion Street (552 6813). Argyle Street or High Street rail. **Meals served** 9am-11.30pm Mon-Sat; noon-11.30pm Sun. **Average** ££. **Credit** AmEx, MC, V.

This cosy bistro, occupying the former site of the city's cheese market, is where Glasgow's Merchant City taste renaissance began back in 1979 – and it has wisely stuck to its winning formula ever since, serving canny Caledonian cuisine to a diverse and loyal clientele. Sculptor Tim Stead's now-iconic wooden furniture and fittings, the barely audible classical music and the friendly but unobtrusive service are all part of its relaxed charm. Gandolfi standards, such as Stornoway black pudding with mushrooms and pancakes, and delicate smoked venison, are legendary. The seasonal menu also lends itself to quirkier combinations, such as seared duck breast topped with plum sauce and crisp fried onions. It's also kind to veggies; the sumptuous gorgonzola, pine nut and red pepper linguine is the king of pasta dishes in a city not short of reputable Italian joints. Breakfasts are hearty, no-nonsense affairs, and somewhat oriented towards the stalwart Scottish scone. While you would be mad to miss such good gastronomic value, Gandolfi is also an ideal setting for coffee and a chinwag. If you're after a light lunch, a coffee or just a

tipple, Gandolfi now has a first-floor bar, serving patrons a stripped-down version of the main menu in a white brick, loft-style environment.

City Merchant Restaurant ★

97 Candleriggs (553 1577/www.citymerchant.co.uk).
Queen Street rail/St Enoch underground. **Meals served** noon-10.30pm Mon-Sat. **Average** ££. **Credit** AmEx, DC, MC, V.

An upmarket, family-run joint with a vaguely Celtic theme to its warm, amber decor, stained glass and wooden floors. They're particularly known for their seafood; daily fish market specials appear both as starters (the seared king scallops with couscous and tomato chilli dressing is particularly refreshing) and mains. There's a set and à la carte menu, both of which feature the odd tacky item – most restaurants have dropped prawn marie rose these days – but the standard of the steaks, haggis and lamb shank is pretty high. A lengthy wine list is backed up by blackboard bin-end bargains, and the staff are quite knowledgeable about recommendations. Popular with business types, it was one of the first restaurants to open in the Merchant City area when it began to be gentrified in the 1980s. The upstairs loft has a gorgeous small private dining area for hire.

Inn on the Green

25 Greenhead Street (554 0165/www.theinnonthegreen. co.uk). Bus 240, 255, 260. **Meals served** noon-2pm, 6-9.30pm Mon-Fri; 7-9.30pm Sat, Sun. **Average** ££. **Credit** AmEx, DC, MC, V.

This place is a real charmer, and a boon for the East End, which is hardly renowned for its culinary delights. Converted from a seamen's mission to a hotel in 1984, the Inn still has a salty-dog feel, but with tartan additions, original art for sale and a grand piano emitting strains of Gershwin, Irving Berlin and… Robbie Williams? Oh well, you can't have everything. Miniature plaques detail the restaurant's celebrity patrons, none of whom is among the hippest young bucks in Scottish media land any more. But its honest-to-goodness Scottish cuisine is as excellent as ever. St Andrew's fillet steak topped with haggis in whisky sauce is Caledonian nirvana, and the fresh Scottish scallops are, thankfully, nothing like the common rubberised variety. To top it all, vanilla and passionfruit cheesecake is a remarkable pud experience. Service is refreshingly low key. Best to get there by taxi.

Rab Ha's ★

83 Hutcheson Street (572 0400). Buchanan Street or St Enoch underground. **Meals served** *Bar* noon-10pm daily. *Restaurant* 5.30-9.30pm daily. **Average** ££. **Credit** AmEx, DC, MC, V.

A bit of history: Rab Ha was a famous Glasgow glutton who ate himself to death in 1843 after a diet that involved gobbling three chickens at once or a whole calf in one meal. No one expects you to follow in his bulky wake, but this cheerfully foodie-centric place is willing to help you try. The restaurant is slightly old-fashioned in design – or perhaps it's a look that's come back into style, who knows? – with touches of tartan. Rab Ha's is known for its haggis (possibly one of the most renowned in the city), but the menu is mostly a mixture of restaurant classics from various genres. The French roast chicken is satisfyingly rich and the soups filling and well-flavoured. There's also a good organic selection, possibly because of sister restaurant Air Organic (*see p188*). The attached bar offers daytime food, which includes some dishes from the restaurant menu, as well as the standard burgers, chips and the like.

Schottische

16-18 Blackfriars Street (552 7774). Buchanan Street underground. **Meals served** *Bar* noon-10pm daily. *Restaurant* 6-9.30pm Wed-Sat. **Average** ££. **Credit** MC, V.

No, not someone with a speech impediment trying to pronounce 'Scottish'; this restaurant is named after a

The **Barras market** – selling food, textiles, bric-a-brac and clothes – offers an essential slice of Glasgow street life every weekend. It's next to the Barrowland ballroom, between Gallowgate and London Road, just east of Glasgow Cross.

German dance influenced by the Highland Fling. But the theme is certainly local enough. This was one of the first places in town really to exploit the new wave in Scots cuisine, proudly casting off the old habits of slavish adherence to French cooking to celebrate the country's own traditions and produce. However, that doesn't mean just mince 'n' tatties: the kitchen takes top-drawer ingredients (venison, seafood, haggis) and cooks them with European techniques to show that Scottish food can be as sophisticated as anything. Dishes on offer change nightly depending on what's in stock and season. The restaurant is upstairs from Babbity Bowster (*see p169*), which also has a café-bar menu.

Russian

Café Cossachok

10 King Street (553 0733). Argyle Street rail. **Meals served** 11am-3pm, 6-11pm Tue, Wed; 11am-11pm Thur-Sat; 3pm-midnight Sun. **Average** ££. **Credit** MC, V.
Funky King Street is where you will find a concentration of Glasgow's independent art galleries, some cool bars and this little gem. Café Cossachok is the culinary and social hub of Glasgow's small Russian community, at least some of whom are guaranteed to be sitting in a corner, tucking into the typically filling Russian cuisine or slamming a flavoured vodka from the generous selection behind the dainty bar. Don't expect the faux Soviet decor you get in vodka theme bars; Cossachok goes for a modern rural look, with simple wooden furniture and a blanket of colourful peasant scarves covering the ceiling, and classic country food to match. Share a *zakuski* (starter) platter of meat (called a Tsar), fish (Tsarina) or veg (Rasputin) before ploughing into mains with slightly naff themed names, such as Chicken Vladimir and Salmon Baikal. Moussaka and blintzes with a variety of potato-oriented fillings are also staples.

Café-bars & Cafés

Ad Lib

111 Hope Street (248 6645). Buchanan Street underground/ Central Station rail. **Open** noon-midnight Mon-Thur; noon-3am Fri, Sat; 1pm-midnight Sun. **Meals served** noon-9.30pm daily. **Average** ££. **Credit** AmEx, MC, V.
From the people who brought you Brel (*see p193*) comes the equally distinctive Ad Lib, situated a stone's throw from Central Station and probably responsible for a good few missed trains in its time. A narrow minimalist bar area leads to the main dining/drinking/clubbing zone;

Coffee, tea and scones

Like every other UK city, even alcohol-friendly Glasgow has gladly succumbed to the steady advance of coffee shop culture. There are numerous branches of Starbucks and Costa Coffee dotted around the city centre and West End, with franchises in the two main train stations. But those seeking a less corporate coffee encounter are spoilt for options, particularly in the West End, where lingering over a latte in a stylish setting is practically an art form.

Tinderbox (189 Byres Road, 339 3108) is ideally located at a major junction and is an established magnet for Byres Road shoppers, students and locals who converge to watch the world go by or check their email. The Vespa scooter in the window is a local landmark, and a symbol of the place's cool, contemporary Italian feel.

Beanscene (5 DeCourcey's Arcade, Cresswell Lane, 334 6776; also with a Southside branch at 19 Skirving Street, 632 8090) is cosier, favouring leather couches and rustic wooden tables. It's a mecca for young mums, and students who don't mind negotiating the pram jam during the day. Local musicians perform acoustically every Thursday night.

Offshore (3-5 Gibson Street, 341 0110), on the other side of the Glasgow University campus, used to be a furniture store and before that a kite shop; now it specialises in teas, coffees and between-meals snacks, and regularly showcases the work of young artists in its basement gallery. City centre haunt **Where The Monkey Sleeps** (see p168) also exhibits local artistic talent.

But perhaps the most bohemian of all is the enormously laid-back **Tchai Ovna** tearoom (42 Otago Lane, 357 4524), which combines charming clutter with a certain Arabian chic. In a sea of teas, their chai latte is recommended. This tiny den has a packed programme of events, from jazz, world and acoustic music sessions to poetry evenings and even the occasional theatrical production.

While these funky, arts-friendly hangouts flourish, the genteel tearoom is fading in prominence, although the Charles Rennie Mackintosh

Ad Lib opens late on weekend nights when they literally push the furniture aside for a boogie to hip hop, house and electro sounds. During the day, light streams in through the glass ceiling (that's the theory, but this is rainy Glasgow) and fronds of greenery complete the conservatory feel. The menu adopts a mix-and-match approach to world cuisine – breads, burgers, pastas and noodle dishes are staples, but there is a daily specials board with tempting alternatives for every course – creamy wild mushroom risotto, anyone? Set aside a few

Glasgow: City centre

industry keeps a couple of stalwarts deservedly afloat. **Miss Cranston's Tearooms** (33 Gordon Street, 204 1122) and the **Willow Tearooms** (217 Sauchiehall Street, 332 0521; 97 Buchanan Street, 204 5242) are painstaking recreations or pastiches of original Mackintosh-designed tearooms serving scones, butteries, thick Scottish pancakes and tea brewed from tea leaves to a constant stream of enthusiastic tourists.

Afternoon tea and cakes has its place in the Scottish psyche, but combine it with the availability of a greasy fry-up and mouth-watering ice-creams and you have the time-honoured recipe for the countless old-fashioned Scots-Italian cafés that can be found all over Scotland, from sleepy coastal resorts to city suburbs.

Almost every district in the city has its own local ice-cream-cum-greasy-spoon-café, although many have expanded their takeaway output to include the ubiquitous pizza/kebab/baked potato options, and lost some of their charm in the process. On the Southside, the **Queen's Park Café** (515-517 Victoria Road, 423 2409), not to be confused with the bar of the same name across the road, and **Café Amalfi** (55 Mount Annan Drive, 632 2814) in Mount Florida preserve the proud tradition of formica table tops and the daddy of ice-cream confections, the knickerbocker glory.

But for the ultimate post-war café time warp, head back to the West End to sample the art deco style of the **University Café** (87 Byres Road, 339 5217). Its budget eats include basic pasta dishes and the classic combo of pie, beans and chips. The café window, dressed in cheap streamers, fake flowers and sample boxes of Milk Tray, is a museum piece in itself.

hours to relax in style, and don't worry about catching that train – there's a taxi rank across the road.

The Arches

253 Argyle Street (565 1035/www.thearches.co.uk).
St Enoch underground. **Open** 11am-midnight daily.
Meals served noon-8.45pm daily. **Average** £. **Credit** AmEx, MC, V.
One of the city's trendiest venues, the Arches is housed by Central Station under the railway arches, which lay

empty for years until they were reopened during the city's term as European City of Culture in 1990. Aptly, it's now an arts venue/bar/café/nightclub, where some of Glasgow's hippest hang out. The eating area is a chilled, white-themed basement room; there's also a bar upstairs for pre-theatre or pre-club drinks, all with low, cube-style seating and polished wooden tables. The food is pretty stylish too, with a nouvelle cuisine sensibility but filling portions; fish, pasta and tortilla wraps are staples. There are also bar snacks, nachos and the like.

Arta

The Old Cheesemarket, 13-19 Walls Street (552 2101/ www.arta.co.uk). Buchanan Street underground. **Open** 5pm-midnight Wed, Thur, Sun; 5pm-3am Fri, Sat. **Meals served** 5-11pm Wed, Thur, Sun; 5pm-midnight Fri, Sat. **Average £. Credit** AmEx, MC, V.
Arta is housed in the Old Cheesemarket building – which is sort of appropriate as there's a cheesy touch to the grandiose decor of this upmarket joint; think Versace-

Budda. *See p162.*

style for such non-subtle touches as huge candelabras, mock antique statuary and Spanish mosaics. You might well see a few Versace outfits on the clientele too, especially in the ground-floor bar, which serves as a gathering place for those going clubbing later. Upstairs, there's a quieter dining area with a menu specialising in tapas and other Spanish dishes, as well as pizza and pasta. The food is much less flashy than the atmosphere, being pleasantly presented and well cooked.

Bargo

80 Albion Street (553 4771). St Enoch underground.
Open noon-midnight Mon-Sat; 12.30pm-midnight Sun.
Meals served noon-7pm Mon-Thur, Sun; noon-8pm Fri,
Sat. **Average** £. **Credit** AmEx, MC, V.
Bargo is definitely a style bar, though it's hard to say just what the style is: it's stylish without being too modish, and if there's a theme, it's low-key industrial. The main feature is the clean-lined glass frontage, through which you can spy a fashionable, twentysomething crowd

gathered around a spacious interior that's decorated with light wood furniture and steel pillars. The bar food is decent if uninspired. A DJ booth in the corner provides the requisite sounds to accompany a night's frolicking.

Budda

408 Sauchiehall Street (332 2010). Charing Cross rail. **Open** *noon-midnight daily.* **Food served** *noon-8pm daily.* **Credit** *MC, V.*

So they can't spell properly; that hasn't stopped Budda expanding from the original St Vincent Street grotto to include branches in the burbs and beyond the city limits. The design theme is eastern Mediterranean/North African

The best takeaways

Coronation Restaurant

55 Gallowgate, City centre (552 3994).
Traditional fish and chip shop handily placed for a takeaway on the way back to town after seeing a gig at Barrowlands.

Crepe e Croissant

Ashley Street, off Woodlands Road, West End (353 2170).
For an alternative to conventional carryouts, this van by the garage offers crêpes with savoury or sweet fillings – chocolate Nutella is very popular – as well as other hot snacks.

Greggs the Baker

13 George Square, City centre (221 0950).
You'll find branches of Greggs all over Glasgow, but this is probably the flagship operation, selling traditional pies, bridies, sausage rolls, doughnuts and more. *See also p64* **Snack attack**.

Little Italy

205 Byres Road, West End (339 6287).
Popular deli/takeaway selling thin, crispy pizza slices and good coffee.

Naked Soup

Fresh ingredients and lots of flavours to take out in stylish pots. *See p196.*

Oxford Fish Restaurant

4 Hill Street, City centre (332 3420).
Classy chippy for a superior supper.

Despite the lousy weather, Glaswegians love ice-cream: excellent local brands include **Crolla**, **Mackie's**, **Nardini's** and **Cream o'Galloway**.

and, apart from some overpowering mosaic tiling in the toilets, it is executed tastefully for a chain venture. No such focus on the menu, however, which adopts a catch-all approach to modern bar food, incorporating soups, sandwiches, nachos and a creamy Thai green curry with sticky rice into its adequate selection. Come the evening, funk, Latin and house music pumps from the speakers and the emphasis shifts to alcohol consumption. Of the two city centre branches, the newer Sauchiehall Street premises are the more spacious, with a dedicated raised dining area at the back, while the smaller subterranean St Vincent Street branch has the cosy, comfy edge, and a club upstairs if you really must stay out.
Branches: 142A St Vincent Street, City centre (221 5660); 16 Algie Street, Southside (636 9171).

Café Cosmo

Glasgow Film Theatre, 12 Rose Street (332 6535).
Cowcaddens underground. **Open** noon-9pm Mon-Sat; 30mins before 1st film-9pm Sun. **No credit cards**.
Most people only pop in here if they're seeing a movie at Glasgow's fantastic little film theatre, but, while it doesn't open that late, Cosmo is a really nice, relaxed and arty place to have a couple of drinks at any time. More or less in keeping with the art deco-ish style of the cinema, it hosts regular painting and photography exhibitions, sometimes with a filmic theme. There's not a great choice of food, but you can pick up snacks such as muffins, cakes and ice-cream. Cosmo is, if anything, even cooler during the day, and a comfortable spot for solo travellers.

Café Hula

321 Hope Street (353 1660). Cowcaddens underground.
Open 9am-11pm Mon-Sat; 10.30am-5pm Sun. **Average** £. **Credit** MC, V.
With its mismatched furniture and random knick-knacks, Café Hula looks like an uncontrived cross between a rustic Mediterranean café and an easygoing bohemian hangout. It has the undisturbed air of a best-kept secret and its patrons probably like it that way, but the management has gradually been upping the profile, extending the opening hours, gaining a licence and introducing a more ambitious menu. By day, passing punters drop by for soup, made-to-order sandwiches or a leisurely coffee to sip while perusing the papers, but in the evening the kitchen cooks up the likes of seared salmon with olive mash or fillet beef with dauphinoise potatoes and caramelised vegetables. International tapas at under £4 per dish include glazed beetroot with feta and toasted pumpkin seeds, and chickpea and chorizo stew. The live music programme, including a traditional Scottish session on Wednesdays and acoustic rock and blues on Fridays, is set to expand.

Glasgow: City centre

Lowdown

158A Bath Street (331 4061). Buchanan Street underground. **Open** noon-1am Mon-Wed, Sun; noon-2am Thur; noon-3am Fri, Sat. **Meals served** noon-11pm daily. **Average** £. **Credit** AmEx, DC, MC, V.

Part of the three-level complex that includes posh restaurant Quigley's (*see p151*) and portentous style joint the Kelly Cooper Bar, this place can stake a claim to be part of the nexus where the city's beautiful people hang out. The Lowdown itself, though, is a discreet basement-level haven with less of the posing and attitude. It's a bit cavernous, which doesn't help the atmosphere at quiet times, but when buzzing it seems to fill up nicely. Big, big tables make it an ideal choice for a large group – they're almost Japanese in feel, square and wooden, with squat, square stools, while dim lighting helps the faintly exotic feel. The food is a cut above most bar fare: there's a good selection of tapas, grouped into Asia, the Mediterranean and the Americas (including tasty creole-spiced fish cakes). There are also soups, wraps and more basic options; the beer-battered cod and thick chips is delicious – but Lowdown loses points for presentation by serving it in a slippy sushi bowl that's a real nuisance.

Mono ★

12 Kings Court, King Street (553 2400/www.gomono. com). St. Enoch underground. **Open** noon-midnight daily. **Meals served** noon-11pm Mon-Sat; 12.30-11pm Sun. **Average** ££. **Credit** MC, V.

This is pretty much the centre of the Glasgow music scene, even though it only opened in late 2002, having been started by the gang who made the 13th Note Café (*see p167*) one of the coolest places in the city. The bright, warehouse-style complex includes a health food/fair trade store and excellent specialist record shop Monorail (indie, psychedelic, punk, soul and other niche genres) as well as the café-bar. Dominated by a large, mosaic-style domed mural on the ceiling, it has a raised eating area and comfy armchairs by the bar, as well as industrial-looking vats by the stone walls. The menu is the only one in Scotland to be exclusively vegan, with no animal, dairy or GM products. It's divided into Side A ('For those about to eat…') for lighter meals such as burgers (deliciously juicy and filling), spicy chips, salads and breakfasts; and Side AA ('We salute you') for inventive mains. No dull dry nutloaf here, but tasty options such as white wine and vegetable casserole with roasted sweet and baby potatoes. Drinks include organic wines and thirst-quenching home-made ginger beer and lemonade-cranberry drinks (1% alcohol). The service is a little slapdash, but terribly friendly. Glasgow indie luminaries like the Delgados and Teenage Fanclub can often be spotted here.

Republic Bier Halle

Republic Bier Halle ★

9 Gordon Street (204 0706/www.republicbierhalle.com).
Buchanan Street underground/Central Station rail.
Open noon-midnight daily. **Food served** noon-10pm
daily. **Average £. Credit** AmEx, DC, MC, V.

This basement bunker has highly individual appeal in
an area of town not noted for taking chances with its
choice of nightlife. Trading since 1999, it specialises in
eastern European beverages and food in a stylised beer
hall environment. The potentially austere backdrop of
concrete walls and boxy wooden tables is softened by
mood lighting and some picturesque alpine friezes. The
back room is particularly cosy, fitted out like a snazzy
penthouse suite from the 1970s. Because of its central
location, it attracts shoppers, workers and clubbers down
its stone steps to soak up the copious varieties of vodka,
schnapps and steins of Czech beer with some excellent

café-style food. Apart from goulash and frankfurters, the menu of soups, pizzas and paninis is not strictly eastern European. One continental convention is adhered to: unless it's really busy, drinks are ordered through a waitress. A second branch, the Republic Bier Stube, opened in the Southside in 2002 (*see p208*).

Sleepless on Sauchiehall Street

415 Sauchiehall Street (332 9290). **Open** 8.30pm-5.30am daily. **Average** £.

OK, the name is a bad, baaaad pun, but this is a really handy joint, so let's forgive them. Situated on the first floor, it's only open at night and it's licensed. In other words, if you've been carousing in the pub all night, but don't want to go clubbing or go home, and you crave some food (and can't face the kebab shops) or another couple of drinks, then here's the answer. Healthy eating options include soups, pasta and rice dishes, but you're more likely to want to get stuck into the burgers, fries (curly and straight varieties), nachos, pancakes, waffles and the like, aimed directly at the post-pub appetite. There's not much atmosphere – the layout is basic and TVs blare out music channels – but it's fun to get a window booth and look down on the less-efficient drunks staggering along Sauchiehall Street, takeaways clutched in hand. Suckers.

Strata

45 Queen Street (221 1888). St Enoch underground.
Open noon-midnight daily. **Meals served** noon-11pm
Mon-Sat; 12.30-11pm Sun. **Average** ££. **Credit** MC, V.
This bar-restaurant makes more of its food than most,
with a Scottish/European slant they describe as 'eclectic'.
It's particularly good for lunch, with light but interesting
meals such as chicken, pineapple and candied ginger
salad, as well as mussels, sandwiches, burgers and more
substantial offerings like steaks. At night there are pre-
theatre and full evening menus, which mix standard
ingredients with unusual dressings and sauces, along
with more innovative dishes such as pigeon breast in port
wine and sultana sauce, and ostrich fillet sautéd with
onions – much nicer than it sounds, honest. The chocolate
bar ice-creams are a joy for those who would otherwise
head for the sweet shop after dinner. The bar, meanwhile
(designed by funky local firms Timorous Beasties and One
Foot Taller), is cool and elegant, and was understandably
named Style Bar of the Year shortly after opening in 2000.
Currently, there's a special cocktail night on Wednesdays,
and DJs at the weekend – which is perhaps a little noisy
for those just wanting a quiet meal.

13th Note Café

50-60 King Street (553 1638/www.13thnote.co.uk).
St Enoch underground/Argyle Street rail. **Open** noon-
midnight daily. **Meals served** noon-10pm daily.
Credit MC, V.
The much loved 13th Note Café changed hands in 2002,
but its new owners have decided that if it ain't broke, why
fix it? The Note is probably best known as a music venue,
so if you choose to visit its vegan café at night, don't be
surprised to see a parade of young punks carting
equipment downstairs or to hear muffled sounds seeping
up through the floorboards from the tiny room where the
stars of tomorrow are born. The look on the far more
spacious ground floor is art-deco-meets-student dive,
while the clientele are probably members of a local indie
band. Generous helpings of hearty vegan wholefood fare
are served in the café section in the back, or you can order
tapas in the main bar. The veggie burgers are celebrated
almost as much as the Note's contribution to the
Glaswegian music scene.

The Universal

57-59 Sauchiehall Lane (332 8899). Charing Cross rail.
Open 11am-midnight daily. **Meals served** *Restaurant*
5-9pm Tue-Thur; 5-10pm Fri, Sat. *Bar* noon-8.30pm daily.
Average *Restaurant* ££. **Credit** MC, V.
This operation, tucked along a bijou cobbled lane
between Renfield Street and Hope Street, originally

Strata

opened as 24-hour café the Lane. The name has changed and the hours have been curtailed, but the Universal – housing a ground-floor bar and a first-floor restaurant and ultra-comfy lounge bar – is still a refreshing addition to a part of town more typically characterised by brash chain establishments catering for big nights out. At the Universal, you're more likely to bump into members of Del Amitri than riotous hen parties. The exposed brick walls and rafters are reminiscent of a New York loft conversion, but without the exclusivity factor. The restaurant menu is not terribly inspired – Cointreau chicken, sirloin steak and wild mushroom and walnut risotto are typical of the mains – but, at £10 for a two-course pre-theatre meal, it is good value. The vibey ground-floor bar (with a separate, extensive menu of lighter bites) plays retro rock classics at optimum volume – not so loud as to encroach on your conversation, but loud enough to get you humming along in recognition.

Where The Monkey Sleeps

182 West Regent Street (226 3406). Cowcaddens or Buchanan Street underground. **Open** 7am-7pm Mon-Fri; 10am-6pm Sat. **Meals served** 7am-6pm Mon-Fri; 10am-6pm Sat. **No credit cards**.

A basement-level coffee bar with a whimsical edge shown through their amusing menus, interesting selection of music and wacky projects: they collect photographs of customers called Dave, for instance, so be prepared to

Babbity Bowster

pose if that's your name. Foreign visitors may also be asked to contribute to the list of translations of the shop's title. The staff do, however, take their coffee seriously, and make it to barista level; there are nice soups and sandwiches too. The small adjoining gallery hosts regularly changing exhibitions.

Pubs & Bars

Babbity Bowster

16-18 Blackfriars Street (552 5055). Queen Street underground. **Open** 11am-midnight Mon-Sat; 10am-midnight Sun. **Credit** AmEx, MC, V.

The most famous part of the townhouse complex that houses a hotel and the Schottische restaurant (*see p156*), Babbity's has for years been a catch-all term for the kind of arty, upmarket hangout that preceded the current style-bar craze. One could be satirical about the certain type of swanky, moneyed bohemian that drinks here, but Babbity's is still highly regarded as an excellent example of Glasgow's classy side, with a dignified history, relaxed sense of humour and little pretension. The bar is cosy, with a fire and an atmosphere aimed at providing the right surroundings for a night of good conversation and, occasionally, good folk music – something that is commemorated in the wall murals of performers and historic Glasgow scenes. The name, incidentally, comes from a traditional country dance that closed the evening at many an old Scots wedding. The food, in keeping with the restaurant upstairs, is a good-quality mixture of Scots and European cuisine, such as oysters and haggis. Drinks include Maclay's 70/- and 80/- ales, as well as guest beers. There's a garden outside for warmer months (or weeks), where you can play boules.

Bar 91

*91 Candleriggs (552 5211). St Enoch underground/
Argyle Street rail.* **Open** 11.30am-midnight daily.
Credit AmEx, DC, MC, V.
Bar 91 is a good-looking bar with dark brick walls, vibrantly coloured upholstery and Peter Howsonesque paintings. The design focal point is the relief sculpture above the bar; supposedly a gigantic wine rack, it looks more like Donald Sutherland's rain machine in Kate Bush's *Cloudbusting* video. You can happily while away hours here: the lighting is low, the atmosphere relaxed, newspapers are supplied, the wine and coffee flows and the Merchant City is your oyster. During the day, do sample the eclectic bar menu, which encompasses Greek, Mexican, Thai and American dishes among others.

Bar 10

10 Mitchell Lane (572 1448). St Enoch underground.
Open 10am-midnight Mon-Sat; noon-midnight Sun.
Credit MC, V.
The first style bar in a city now heaving with vogue drinking dens, Bar 10 has seen changes in the area in its 13 years – not least the construction of the Lighthouse museum directly across the lane – while retaining its pull on the clubbing crowd. When it opened in 1990, Glasgow had never seen anything like its minimalist industrial look, designed by style guru Ben Kelly (also responsible for Manchester's Dry Bar and the late lamented Hacienda); nowadays it's hard to recall a time when Bar 10 was not around to serve the funky set with tasty sandwiches and snacks during the day and DJ sets during weekend nights.

Blackfriars

36 Bell Street (552 5924). Buchanan Street or St Enoch underground. **Open** noon-midnight Mon-Sat; 12.30pm-midnight Sun. **Credit** AmEx, MC, V.
Blackfriars is a Merchant City staple with a dark, traditional look (cheered, though, by entertainment posters on most walls), attracting a lively weekend crowd. The inside is dark, with a long bar, and candles on wooden tables that create an intimate air. There are plenty of real ales, with the likes of Belhaven, Caledonian and Houston, and Belgian beers on tap. The food is

Glasgow's **Chinatown** is tiny, but it does have a small shopping and restaurant complex – and a traditional arch – at New City Road, by the motorway behind Cowcaddens.

standard bar fare – though fairly satisfying: own-made soup, bangers 'n' mash, burgers and pizza. There's also a neat little downstairs bar with a dancefloor, which hosts occasional small clubs and gigs.

Candy Bar

185 Hope Street (353 7420). Buchanan Street underground. **Open** noon-midnight daily. **Credit** AmEx, MC, V.

Not a confectioner's fantasy haunt, but a sleek style bar with a retro feel. The functional dark wood panelling and leather-fronted curved bar conjure up images of groovy party scenes in some swinging '60s flick and, should you be brave enough to sample the Champagne Candynova (a pitcher of vodka, peach schnapps, champagne and fresh orange juice), it won't be long before you start seeing your own swirling, psychedelic shapes. Candy Bar is frequented by a youngish post-work, pre-club drinking crowd who cluster round the window seats to see and be seen. Exotic sandwiches, salads, noodles and pasta dishes are served until 8pm.

The Horseshoe

17 Drury Street (229 5711). Buchanan Street underground/Central Station rail. **Open** 11am-midnight Mon-Sat; 12.30pm-midnight Sun. **Credit** AmEx, MC, V.

The Horseshoe

Boozing by Underground

I belong to Glasgow
Dear old Glasgow toon
There's something the matter
wi' Glasgow
Cos it's goin' roon' an' roon'

The Glaswegian predilection for hard liquor is immortalised in traditional song, but also evident on any Saturday night in Sauchiehall Street. Fortunately, the city's reputation for drunken rabble-rousing has given way to a friendlier, sociable image – and it would be a shame not to partake of such hospitality, particularly with such a varied drinking scene to choose from. The more adventurous and doughty drinker should consider tackling the 'subcrawl', a mammoth pub crawl based on the 15 stops of the Glasgow Underground circle (aka the 'Clockwork Orange' because of the colour of the trains).

The idea is simple: buy yourself a Discovery day pass for the Underground, alight at the first station you come to and have a drink in a neighbourhood pub, head back to the tube, repeat the process – until you complete the circuit or fall over, whichever happens first. The starting point is entirely at the discretion of individual crawlers, but the stops on the south of the river – Bridge Street to Govan – are best attempted first, while your group still retains basic motor functions. These areas are worlds apart from the more refined districts north of the Clyde. In fact, it's best to skip a couple of stations at this stage and save your liver for the more congenial selection of hostelries at the West End and city centre stops.

Set aside a few hours – ten should do it – to complete the crawl. Bear in mind that the Underground shuts soon after 11pm (6pm on a Sunday), but

The Horseshoe is a true Glasgow landmark with a number of bizarre claims to fame. It has the longest continuous bar in Europe, for one thing – a curved Victorian circle that is usually mobbed by people determined to assert themselves as characters (particularly if there happens to be a Rangers game on TV). Its regular and hugely popular karaoke sessions launched one Gary Mullen to *Stars In Their Eyes* success as a Freddie Mercury soundalike, as a plaque proudly boasts. Scots rockers Travis (back when they were known as Glass Onion) began rehearsing here and later donated a gold disc. It's the kind of place where lunchtime legends are made. The decor is beyond style, beyond tradition: authentic fixtures and fittings, faded photos, nicotine-stained walls (this place is smoky, and coughing politely will have virtually no effect). The food counter in the upstairs lounge is renowned for its

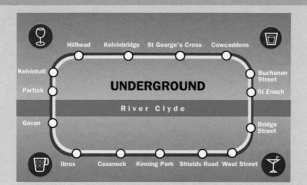

Hillhead Kelvinbridge St George's Cross Cowcaddens

Kelvinhall

Partick

Govan

UNDERGROUND

River Clyde

Buchanan Street

St Enoch

Bridge Street

Ibrox Cessnock Kinning Park Shields Road West Street

you should never have to wait more than five minutes for a train. A subcrawl might go something like this:

Begin at **St Enoch** station, a good central location with a number of bars to choose from. **The Arches** (*see p159*), a funky arts venue so called because it occupies the arches beneath Central Station, has

an excellent café-bar where you can enjoy a civilised glass of wine and line your stomach before tackling the Southside wastelands.

Hop back on the tube and head to the next stop, **Bridge Street**. There are a number of old man's bars in the vicinity, but it's better to take a short walk to **Sharkey's** ▶

cheapness; a three-course lunch costs less than £3 – so haute cuisine isn't on the menu, but if you want a real taste of satisfying Scottish stodge, don't miss it.

King Tut's Wah Wah Hut

272A St Vincent Street (221 5279). Charing Cross rail.
Open noon-midnight Mon-Sat; 6pm-midnight Sun.
Credit (food only) MC, V.
Renowned in rock and pop lore as the venue where Oasis were first spotted and signed ten years ago, King Tut's has also hosted early concerts by Pulp, Blur, Radiohead and local heroes Travis, and was recently voted the UK's best venue by Radio 1 listeners, so it's worth sampling if you are at all interested in new music. Inevitably, the clientele in the basement bar varies from night to night, depending on who's playing the hallowed upstairs room. The pool table and a jukebox groaning

Boozing by Underground
(continued)

▶ (51 Old Rutherglen Road, 429 3944) in the heart of the Gorbals. This area is undergoing regeneration at the moment, but this trusty Irish bar remains impervious to change.

Skip the **West Street** stop – it's all rundown warehouses round here – and make for **Shields Road**. Duck under the M8 and you'll come out on the Paisley Road. The **Old Toll Bar** (1-3 Paisley Road West, 429 3135) is a handsome mix of old and new, dominated by eight unused old whisky barrels over the bar, which are listed artefacts.

Bypass **Kinning Park**, as the selection of public houses in this locale is none too good. But in the interests of sticking to the programme, you should stop at **Cessnock**, where the trad but unremarkable **Kensington Bar** (408 Paisley Road West, 427 3328) is your

best, indeed only, option. **Ibrox** station should also be bodyswerved. Ibrox stadium is the home ground of Rangers FC, so practically every pub in the vicinity is a monument to the club.

The next stop is **Govan**, once the hub of Glasgow's proud shipbuilding industry, now a fairly rundown district that has seen better days. Your watering hole here is the **Brechin Bar** (803 Govan Road, 445 1349), which looks far nicer outside than in.

On crossing under the river to the perky parish of **Partick**, your choice multiplies about a hundredfold, but the **Hayburn Vaults** (427-429 Dumbarton Road, 339 1240) is the handiest hostelry. Next, **Kelvinhall** station at Partick Cross is on the cusp of West End bohemia, so head to style bar the **Living Room** (see p195).

---

with all the current hip sounds are ancillary attractions, while the lunches and bar snacks are popular with the local business crowd.

McChuills

40 High Street (552 2135). Buchanan Street underground.
Open noon-midnight Mon-Sat; 12.30pm-midnight Sun.
Credit MC, V.
An unusual kind of bar, in Glasgow at least, with an emphasis on music visible in its classic album sleeves hanging on the walls (good for playing a game of 'how many have *you* got?' on nights when conversation flags) and complemented by live local bands at weekends and midweek jazz. Watch your head on the low arches that loosely divide the bar area. Each 'section' is similarly dark and cavernous; although the bar is on the ground floor, it's got a basement feel to it, as the long, narrow entrance

Hillhead station in the middle of Byres Road boasts an embarrassment of drinking riches, but, rather than be overwhelmed by choice, just turn right into Ashton Lane and straight into the **Wee Bar Under The Chip**, a snug wee annexe of the wonderful **Ubiquitous Chip** restaurant (*see p192*), which is known colloquially as the Microchip and is probably the best bar in the entire city. You might want to think about eating something at this point too.

Kelvinbridge is a slightly quieter and altogether more sophisticated neighbourhood. A good imbibing choice near the station is the classy but unpretentious wine bar/café **Oblomov** (*see p196*). From here, you can easily walk to the cheap and cheerful **Wintersgills** (226 Great Western Road, 332 3532) – but that would

be cheating, so take the tube to **St George's Cross**.

You are now on the home straight. **Cowcaddens** station is close to city centre civilisation, so take advantage and visit the stylish, youthful **Brunswick Cellars** (239 Sauchiehall Street, 331 1820), complete with kitsch fish tank.

Only one stop remains: **Buchanan Street**. Several possibilities rear their head near the station, but, for some unfathomable reason, huge faux Irish chain pubs always seem to do the business, so put your feet up in **Waxy O'Connors** (43 West George Street, 354 5154). There's even a pizza takeaway place next door to satiate the traditional post-pub munchies.

For further information and a right good Glasgow laugh, read the expert testimony of dedicated subcrawlers at www.subcrawl.co.uk.

doesn't let in much light. The bar menu is a cheerfully random selection of pub grub, Asian and cajun dishes and seafood, served at shaky wooden tables lit by candles in bottles, and at prices that explain the regular student punters, some of whom almost treat it as an extension of the halls of residence canteen.

Nice'n'Sleazy ★

421 Sauchiehall Street (333 9637). Charing Cross rail. **Open** 11.30am-11.45pm daily. **No credit cards**.
Don't be put off by the awful name (it's an old Stranglers song); Sleazys, as its loyal punters call it, is a riot of colourful decor and even more colourful characters who have helped to establish this buzzing bar – advantageously located directly across from the Garage club venue – as the essential hangout for the alternative music crowd. The fact that it boasts its own subterranean

venue, which promotes local bands on a nightly basis, helps enhance its scuzzy, underground appeal. The jukebox is without parallel in the city, provided you enjoy uncompromising punked-up sounds, and the ciabatta pizzas offer all the stomach-lining you'll need.

The Scotia

112 Stockwell Street (552 8681). St Enoch underground/ Argyle Street rail. **Open** 11am-midnight daily. **Food served** noon-5pm daily. **No credit cards**.

The legendary Scotia claims to be the oldest bar in the city; it's certainly an institution that values heritage, from the pictures of old Glasgow and memorabilia adorning the walls to its preservation of the hallowed Scottish traditions of hospitality, conversation and debate – stimulated by good beer and whisky, naturally. With its low roof, beamed ceiling and numerous nooks and crannies, and its spontaneous folk jam sessions and blues band residencies, the Scotia could almost be a tourist board ad for Scottish pub life, were it not so uncontrived.

Variety Bar ★

401 Sauchiehall Street (332 4449). Charing Cross rail. **Open** 11am-midnight Mon-Sat; 12.30pm-midnight Sun. **No credit cards**.

Situated a few doors along from Nice'n'Sleazy (*see p175*), Variety Bar is like the older, cooler cousin who doesn't have to try too hard. Its art deco interior, with stucco walls, ceiling fans and lights that resemble giant peppermint drops, exudes the seedy glamour of an American gin joint from a noir movie. Instead of Bogart, your drinking compadres will be old men in flat caps by day and Art School students and other scenesters by night. The Variety recently changed hands, but its new proprietors have been careful to preserve the bar's singular appeal. And that includes the cheese toasties.

The Victoria Bar ★

157-159 Bridgegate (552 6040). St Enoch underground/ Argyle Street rail. **Open** 11am-midnight Mon-Sat; 12.30pm-midnight Sun. **No credit cards**.

Along with the Scotia (*see above*) and the Clutha Vaults (167 Stockwell Street, 552 7520), the Victoria Bar is part of the 'Stockwell Triangle', where people have been known to disappear after a few too many pale ales. Time becomes a relative concept when you get sucked into the cosy ambience of this traditional snug bar, with an even snugger lounge where acoustic guitars appear by osmosis and the staff and actors from the Citizens Theatre, situated just over the river, congregate to wind down. There's culture, live music, an array of fine malts and, if that's not enough to make you fall in love with this exceptional pub, classic local cuisine: pie and beans for under a quid.

Glasgow: West End

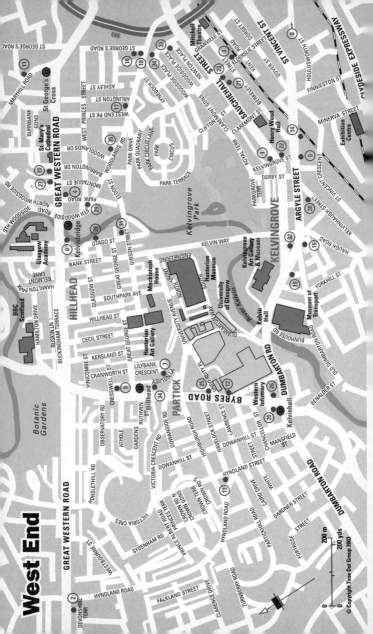

The West End is ubiquitously known as 'Glasgow's trendy West End' by cliché-dependent tabloid journos – but they do have a point. By far the most bohemian part of the city, it mixes shabby student-chic around the university area of Hillhead with posher establishments catering to the wealthier suburban crowd. It's also one of the most cosmopolitan areas of Glasgow, with a large Asian population, reflected in a good range of international cuisine. Compact and convenient for getting around, it's quieter than the city centre at night and, for all its occasional pretentiousness, has an endearing community feel that ensures some residents hardly ever leave its confines.

Restaurants

American

The Cottier

93-5 Hyndland Street (357 5825/www.thecottier.com).
Hillhead or Kelvinhall underground. **Meals served**
noon-4pm, 5-10pm daily. **Average** ££. **Credit** AmEx,
MC, V.
A unique fixture of the West End, Cottier's is housed in a converted church, which also hosts a bar and theatre venue. The restaurant on the first floor – where the

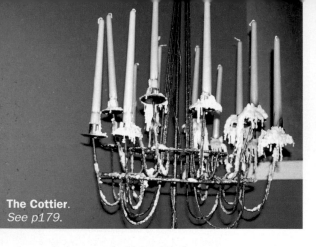

The Cottier.
See p179.

rectory used to be – serves food that could be the answer to your prayers: a mixture of South, Latin and North American flavours with an emphasis on sophisticated, but not pretentious, eating; the red snapper with sweet potato mash is particularly successful. Decorated simply, with wide tables and plain walls, there's not much to distract you from the food; the atmosphere could even be said to be a little chilly, though it's usually pretty busy. Downstairs, the bar is one of the most gorgeous in Glasgow, with the church's stained glass, high beams and ornate carvings intact, as well as pew-style booths. There's a decent bar menu (burgers, fat chips and the like) and regular jazz sessions that are popular with families. Cottier's outdoor beer garden really comes into its own in summer when it's mobbed with the West End's hippest, but all year round it's a pretty trendy joint beloved by artsy types and students.

Asian

The Ashoka

108 Elderslie Street (221 1761). Charing Cross rail.
Meals served noon-2pm, 5pm-midnight Mon-Sat; 5pm-midnight Sun. **Average** ££. **Credit** AmEx, DC, MC, V.

It's easy to get confused when it comes to Glasgow's many curry restaurants, some of which have very similar names – but this Ashoka is not, in fact, related to the others of the same name around the West End owned by the Harlequin chain. Dating back to 1978, this one really kick-started the whole trend, and has a loyal local clientele. The grandly opulent decor is largely traditional, and the menu presents the usual Indian and Kashmiri

Glasgow's farmers' market takes place on the second and fourth Saturday of the month (10am-3pm) at Mansfield Park, Partick. Details on 01738 449430.

dishes, plus some unusual ones – fruit pakora in batter, for instance. They're proud of their special 'abpaz' cooking technique, which involves flash-frying meat to seal in the juices before adding sauces. There's also a good takeaway menu. A rather trendier offshoot, Ashoka Flame, recently opened in the basement.

Chow

98 Byres Road (334 9818). Hillhead underground. **Open** noon-2pm, 5-11pm Mon-Sat; 4.30-11pm Sun. **Average** ££. **Credit** AmEx, MC, V.

Chow has followed the example of other minimalist noodle shops in the city and opted for a zen-like interior decor to maximise its intimate space. There are only ten tables over two floors and, given the restaurant's prime location on the West End's main shopping drag, they are regularly filled. However, the service is fast and efficient enough to accommodate a high turnover of patrons, whether sampling the £6.50 three-course lunch or checking in for dinner. Start with crispy noodles in spicy egg sauce or yuk sung, a lettuce wrap. Mains include noodle soups, fried rice dishes, chow meins, seasonal fare such as crayfish, and chicken, beef, seafood or vegetarian dishes that can be cooked 'Tam's style' (with a garlic and bean sauce on deep-fried rice noodles, with a sprinkling of sesame seeds on top) or 'touban' (peppers and onion in a spicy tomato sauce). And if they can't fit you in, there's always the takeaway service as a consolation.

Creme de la Creme

1071 Argyle Street (221 3222). Exhibition Centre rail. **Meals served** noon-midnight Mon-Fri; 2pm-midnight Sat; 5pm-midnight Sun. **Average** ££. **Credit** AmEx, DC, MC, V.

Miss Jean Brodie's favourite description of her Edinburgh schoolgirl acolytes is more commonly associated with big-value Indian food in Glasgow. Creme de la Creme is not everyone's idea of top of the popadoms; some find it too expansive and impersonal, though, unlike other vast eateries, it has bags of character, retaining many of the design features from its former life as an art deco cinema. (If only a Wurlitzer organ would rise through the floor to accompany the consumption of pakora.) The main attraction for its regular clientele is the buffet served nightly in the balcony area, allowing as many helpings of Indian faves as the belly can handle. The à la carte menu is packed with curry staples, plus specialities such as aloo mazadar (a starter – sticks of fried bread with a cheese and potato filling), lamb with port and cream sauce, and sabas, a buttery green curry with broccoli, spinach and other green vegetables, which is also available in a meat or fish incarnation.

Glasgow: West End

Mother India ★

28 Westminster Terrace, off Sauchiehall Street
(221 1663). Exhibition Centre rail/bus 16, 18, 42.
Meals served noon-2.30pm, 5.30-10.30pm Mon-Thur;
noon-11pm Fri; 1-11pm Sat; 1-10pm Sun. **Average** £.
Credit AmEx, MC, V.

You won't find the all-too-familiar tikka masala experience of the processed and radioactive variety here; Mother India offers authentic Indian home cooking at its best. The city's curry lovers have clearly taken the place to their hearts: this former tearoom in a Sauchiehall Street terrace is often packed out. The first-floor restaurant has a faded Raj air, with the original Victorian opulence smothered by the sheer mass of velvet curtains, candles and bare oak tables. Downstairs, there's more of a modern, bijou brasserie feel. Either way, it's the food that's the star. All the dishes are made to order, and the result is a palpable freshness and subtlety (though you

The Curry Mile

If there is one local delicacy Glaswegians know how to wolf down in profligate quantities, it's a piping bowl of aromatic curry. Some may quibble at the strict geographical accuracy of the description 'local', but consuming a korma, tucking into a tikka or 'going for a Ruby Murray', to use the west coast rhyming slang, is a far more widespread Scottish pursuit than addressing a haggis.

Life in a cold, damp climate automatically lends itself to the comfort eating of hearty, piquant food, and Scotland has a large, vibrant Asian community willing to share the finer points of Indian cuisine with the rest of the population, who are as happy to hoover up vast quantities of takeaway pakora and chips smothered in curry sauce as they are to dine in style. For years, Glasgow has

competed with Birmingham and Bradford for the title of curry capital of the UK, but for Glaswegians there is no debate – their city really is a curry house paradise.

Some of the best are located along a strip, unofficially dubbed the Curry Mile, running from Sauchiehall Street, the hub of city centre nightlife, to Kelvingrove, the height of West End culture. This taste trail begins at the traditional, and late-opening, **Rawalpindi** (319-321 Sauchiehall Street, 332 4180) and the modern **Kama Sutra** (pictured; *see p140*), which occupy the same block in the heart of town.

A brief diversion off the main drag at Charing Cross brings you to **Café India** (171 North Street, 248 4074) – said to have been a favourite of the late Scottish First Minister Donald Dewar (nicknamed may wait a little longer than usual). Many make the pilgrimage for the vegetarian menu; the dosas with various fillings are almost worth the trip in themselves.

Mr Singh's India

149 Elderslie Street (204 0186). Charing Cross rail.
Meals served noon-midnight Mon-Sat; 2.30pm-midnight Sun. **Average** ££. **Credit** AmEx, DC, MC, V.
To many Glaswegians, this is curry paradise. The sated customers in the impressive photo gallery at the entrance include sporting heroes Larsson, McCoist and Souness, not to mention Sir Sean. But we're not talking about some exclusive old boys' curry club; Mr Singh's India is an infectiously friendly, modern restaurant. Staff in kilts whirl around cheerily serving some of the most flavoursome Punjabi dishes in the country, not least the delicate lamb ambala and the chicken tikka with garlic chilli. Vegetarians are equally well catered for – brie

'Donnie Two-Lunches' for his prodigious appetite) – and the opulent **Koh-I-Noor** (225-235 North Street, 221 1555). Just around the corner, **Karisma** (573-581 Sauchiehall Street, 226 5030) is a spacious, traditional restaurant, while the **Shenaz** (17 Granville Street, 221 8528) is a block away, just by the Mitchell Theatre.

Two of the city's favourites, the **Ashoka** (*see p180*) and **Mr Singh's India** (*see above*), where the Indian waiters wear kilts, lie on Elderslie Street, the latter on the corner of Sauchiehall Street. A few Victorian terraces further on is ever-popular **Mother India** (*see above*), as homely and bountiful as its name.

The home straight is just a short walk away on the West End stretch of Argyle Street, starting with **Creme de la Creme** (*see p181*) – unmissable as it is housed in a former art deco cinema – and ending (hopefully with a creamy coffee and chocolate mints) at the adventurous **Spice Of Life** (1293 Argyle Street, 337 6378) and the charming **Ashoka West End** (1284 Argyle Street, 339 3371).

Glasgow: West End

pakora, anyone? Family parties and groups feature prominently, and the staff will be quick to spot and indulge a special celebration.

Shish Mahal

66-68 Park Road (339 8256). Kelvinbridge underground. **Meals served** noon-2pm, 5-11pm Mon-Thur; noon-11.30pm Fri, Sat; 5-11pm Sun. **Average** ££. **Credit** AmEx, MC, V.

The Shish Mahal is the city's longest serving curry house, operating 'since 1964', as proclaimed on the sign over the door. The restaurant has moved location over the years and, judging by the plush modern decor, moved with the times too. The fresh white tablecloths contrast with the deep red upholstery to create an open, comfortable and contemporary environment in which to enjoy some old-school Indian cuisine, and plenty of it. If you need guidance, take heed of the comprehensive, mouth-watering descriptions that accompany each section. House specialities include chilli and garlic nishilee, a masala-style dish, and mashedar, a Punjabi bhuna – but that's just a drop in the Ganges of what's on offer.

Thai Fountain

2 Woodside Crescent (332 1599/www.thai-fountain.com). Charing Cross rail. **Meals served** noon-2.30pm, 5.30-11.30pm Mon-Fri; noon-11.30pm Sat. **Average** £££. **Credit** AmEx, MC, V.

With the Glaswegian fondness for fiery foods, it's surprising that the city is so modestly served with Thai restaurants. But Thai Fountain's longstanding reputation ensures that there will always be patrons willing to seek out this refined establishment, situated in a Georgian tenement beside Charing Cross and just below the once exclusive address of Park Circus. It's a favourite destination for entertaining business clients, but you don't need an expense account budget to enjoy the array of regional red and green curries, spicy salads and tom yum soups – particularly between 5pm and 7.30pm (before 6.30pm on Saturdays), when main courses are half-price. Speciality starters include ka bueong talay (crab meat wrapped in rice flour skins) and kanon bueong youn (crispy pancakes with chicken and coconut). Seafood fans should sample the main course of squid with garlic, chillies, pepper and lemongrass.

Mediterranean

Amaryllis ★

1 Devonshire Gardens (337 3434). Bus 66. **Meals served** noon-2.30pm, 6.45-10.30pm Wed-Fri, Sun; 6.45-10.30pm Sat. **Average** ££££. **Credit** AmEx, MC, V.

Amaryllis

Don't expect simply to turn up and get a table: this hugely successful French restaurant, run by bona fide celebrity chef Gordon Ramsay – the first Scot to win three Michelin stars – often has waiting lists of up to three months. But it may be worth it, for the quality of the eating experience is as high as you'd expect. Housed in the graceful classical dining room of one of Glasgow's most exclusive hotels, everything about Amaryllis says luxury treat. The prix-fixe menu features subtle modernist dishes, such as venison with braised parsnips and carrots with bitter chocolate sauce. The divinely decadent desserts are hard to resist, and the wine list is also fabulous, though pricey. Definitely a venue to take someone you wish to impress or spoil. You'll have a better chance of getting in at short notice at lunchtime.

Café Andaluz
2 Cresswell Lane (339 1111). Hillhead underground.
Meals served noon-11pm Mon-Sat; noon-10.30pm Sun.
Average £. **Credit** AmEx, DC, MC, V.
A recent addition to the behind-Byres Road stretch of restaurants and cafés and an instant hit, this fine tapas joint was set up by the people behind the long-established and very popular local Italian chain Di Maggio's. If Café Andaluz is their attempt to set up a new franchise, it's done with just as much professionalism but rather more imagination. It certainly looks authentic enough: the rich dark wood, bright mosaic tiles and luxurious cushions come, apparently, straight from Spain. Various approaches are possible: you can have just one course, or starters followed by a paella or the special (meat and seafood crop up often), or a big selection of tapas to share,

Renowned Edinburgh cheesemonger **Iain J Mellis** also has a branch in Glasgow, at 492 Great Western Road (339 8998).

with a little rest between servings. The attentive staff have some suggestions if you're not sure, and there are plenty of veggie options. Don't miss the chocolate and seville orange mousse – it's just divine.

Café Cherubini

360 Great Western Road (334 8894). Kelvinbridge underground. **Meals served** 9am-5pm Mon-Wed; 9am-10pm Thur-Sun. **Average £. No credit cards.**

Cherubini is what they'd call in Noo Yoik a 'neighbourhood' place; its exterior (which makes heavy use of, yes, cherubs) hides a family atmosphere that is a draw for Italo-Scots and locals. It's worth a visit if you're nearby: it's a lovely little café with a relaxing vibe, usually playing dreamy, nostalgic music. Tuck into wholesome, old-fashioned Italian dishes – soup, lasagne, chicken cacciatore, tiramisu, salads – just like Tony Soprano's

Air Organic. *See p188.*

mama used to make. It's cheap, too, with a three-course special for £9.95 and main courses no more than £6. The famous Nardini ice-cream makes a delicious finish to lunch or dinner, while the espressos are high quality.

Café du Sud

8-10 Clarendon Street (332 2054). St George's Cross underground. **Meals served** 6pm-midnight Tue-Sat. **Average** ££. **Credit** MC, V.

A lovely, wee, family-run restaurant slightly off the beaten track that combines Provençal and classic French cuisine. Small, intimate and very friendly, it has an endearingly casual atmosphere. Richly painted on the outside, it's candle-lit and very French indoors and a good choice for a romantic night out. The food is excellently pungent and nicely presented, with the likes of roast red pepper mousse with baby spinach, parmesan and pine kernels, or duck cassoulet in a rich red wine and bean ragout. Plenty of nice French wines too. The owners also run the more Italian Bistro du Sud, which caters mainly to a lunchtime and weekend crowd.

Branch: Bistro du Sud 87 Cambridge Street, City centre (332 2666).

Kooks

1355 Argyle Street (334 9682). Kelvinhall underground. **Meals served** noon-9pm Mon-Thur, Sun; noon-10pm Fri, Sat. **Average** ££. **Credit** MC, V.

Named after a song from David Bowie's *Hunky Dory* album, this cosy bistro was opened in 2001 by the team behind city-centre drinking den of iniquity Nice'n'Sleazy (*see p175*). The two establishments share a bohemian outlook, but similarities end there. Where Sleazy's is loud, colourful and crawling with specimens from Glasgow's musical underbelly, Kooks is tasteful and intimate, with low lighting and a sparing Middle Eastern/North African theme to its decor. The pan-European evening menu can range from Stornoway black pudding to Greek meze platters, while the daytime clientele of ladies who lunch and assorted beatniks fill up with a bowl of Kooks' soup or a Sunday roast. The toilets, papered entirely with the pages of old books and comics, are a quirky embellishment, but the main selling point is the classic view, rendered by many an artist, of Kelvingrove Art Gallery with Glasgow University rising behind it.

Middle Eastern

The Bay Tree

403 Great Western Road (334 5898). Kelvinbridge underground. **Meals served** 9am-10pm Mon-Sat; 9am-9pm Sun. **Average** £. **No credit cards.**

Originally a terribly worthy vegan wholefood joint, this little café now offers an unusual Turkish/Greek/Persian/Lebanese menu. In fact, it's probably the only place in Glasgow that offers not just a traditional fry-up, but also an 'Arabian full breakfast'. Some of the dishes are more slapdash than stylish, but they're filling and inexpensive. You'll also find 'happy meals' for kids and some unusual desserts – and there's still a wide range of non-meat choices (cooked separately). Home to numerous West End students over the years, the Bay Tree's funniest claim to fame is a link with *Pop Idol*'s Darius, whose signed photo grins cheesily behind the counter.

Modern European

Air Organic

36 Kelvingrove Street (564 5200). Exhibition Centre rail. **Meals served** noon-10pm Mon-Thur, Sun; noon-10.30pm Fri, Sat. **Average ££. Credit** AmEx, MC, V.

An inventive menu that uses only organic produce is just part of the appeal of Air Organic, a funky, futuristic restaurant and bar situated a block from Kelvingrove Park. Its off-white and ecru decor and space age furniture were the hippest thing going when it opened in the mid '90s. Since then, many have copied but few have captured the place's groovy, 1960s airport lounge ambience. The menu, divided into earth, flora, ocean and carnivore sections, looks like an airline ticket, but there is nothing of the synthetic in-flight meal about the prawn and lemon linguine, barbecue sticky pork salad with mango and jumbo cashews, or pan-fried chicken breast with creamy chive mash. The ground floor bar is an attraction in its own right, offering an assortment of superior sandwiches and pizzas, plus specialities such as organic beefburger and red Thai watermelon curry, to a fashionable but casual student and club-bound crowd.

Scottish

The Buttery ★

652 Argyle Street (221 8188). St Enoch underground. **Meals served** noon-2pm, 7-9.30pm Tue-Thur; noon-2pm, 6-10pm Fri; 6-10pm Sat. **Average ££££. Credit** AmEx, DC, MC, V.

The grand old lady of Glaswegian dining (dating back in some form or other to 1869), this solidly respectable scion of the establishment recently survived a threatened closure. Housed in a traditional tenement in what is nowadays a quiet area, its dining room decor is sombre, dark and elegant, all stiff white tablecloths and crystal glasses. There's also a cocktail bar and a small room for

Hand-prepared 'ready meals' are available at upmarket deli **Heart Buchanan** (380 Byres Road, 334 7626). It's run by Fiona Buchanan, former PA to celeb chef Nick Nairn.

Nairns

discreet parties. The menu is firmly posh Scottish nosh, with the finest local ingredients (cullen skink, Aberdeen Angus, Arbroath smokies and so on) in unthreatening but masterfully prepared dishes. It's expensive to have dinner here, but it's certainly the sort of place where you can see where the money goes: sheer luxury.

Nairns ★

13 Woodside Crescent (353 0707/www.nairns.co.uk). St George's Cross underground. **Meals served** noon-1.45pm, 6-9.45pm Tue-Sat. **Average £££. Credit** AmEx, DC, MC, V.

Nick Nairn really kick-started the whole celeb-chef eaterie deal in Glasgow when he opened this small basement restaurant in a glorious Park Circus Victorian terrace in 1997. Its reputation remains undiminished, though Nairn isn't in the kitchen much anymore. Despite his fame (he studied under Marco Pierre White and was the youngest Scottish chef to win a Michelin star), this is no gimmicky spin-off, but a solidly impressive and classy joint. Top dishes in the frequently changing set dinner (£24.50 for two courses, £29.50 for three) include Thai risotto cake with lemon and soy dressing, a lovely, tart counterpoint to the full-bodied fleshiness of the seared scallops it accompanies, while the char-grilled ribeye, herb mash and roast root vegetables is refreshingly simple and hearty. The lunch set menus are simpler and cheaper, and there's a hefty, if expensive, wine selection. Booking essential.

No.16

16 Byres Road (339 2544). Kelvinhall underground.
Meals served noon-2.30pm, 5.30-10pm Mon-Sat; 12.30-9pm Sun. **Average** ££. **Credit** MC, V.
No.16 doesn't look like much from the outside, what with its nondescript name and tiny size, but this classy joint has been consistently praised by restaurant critics and is usually bursting at the seams (though that's not difficult). The waiting staff are adept at squeezing past the cramped wooden tables, but these are so close together that this isn't the best place to discuss state secrets. The food is the draw: well-cooked, well-presented takes on elegant combinations. Seafood is a particular standout, while the roast chicken breast in madeira sauce is creamily delicious. There's a good wine list too and deliciously tasty sticky toffee pudding, which is hard to resist. Booking recommended.

Stravaigin ★

28 Gibson Street (334 2665). Kelvinbridge underground.
Meals served *Restaurant* 5-11pm Tue-Thur; noon-2.30pm, 5-11pm Fri, Sat; 12.30-2.30pm, 5-11pm Sun.

The Ubiquitous Chip. *See p192.*

Madeleine Valente

Jim Murray

Dave Byrne

Elaine Knox

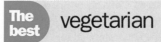

The best vegetarian

The Bay Tree
No longer exclusively veggie, but still offers a selection of meat-free dishes to keep its old punters happy. *See p187.*

Grassroots Café
Hippy haven of all things wholefood and healthy. *See p194.*

Mono
Scotland's only eating establishment that's entirely vegan, dairy-free and GM additive-shunning. *See p164.* Its West End sister, **Stereo** (*see p199*), also has a vegan menu, and regular live music.

Peking Inn
A fine Chinese restaurant with a separate menu for non-meat eaters. *See p143.*

13th Note Café
Simple veggie dishes in a cool atmosphere in this popular music venue. *See p167.*

Café-bar 11am-11pm Mon-Thur; 11am-midnight Fri, Sat; 12.30-11pm Sun. **Average** *Restaurant* £££. **Credit** AmEx, DC, MC, V.

A festoon of AA rosettes and a few restaurant-of-the-year awards adorn this Gibson Street stalwart, one of the daddies of them all when it comes to great local food with an exotic twist. 'Think globally, eat locally' is the Stravaigin mantra, taking good Scottish produce and plunging it into exotic combinations, such as West Coast mussels with sweet chilli, coriander and oyster sauce. The bare yet cosy basement has the feel of an old ship's cabin, while the bar upstairs also offers superior pub grub (fab fish and chips). At Stravaigin's offspring, Stravaigin 2 (*The Times'* Jonathan Meades voted it one of his best three restaurants in Scotland), there's a modern, clean look of polished wood and big windows. The adventurous menu includes a good choice of tapas and a seafood cocktail described as 'Pacific Mexico meets Kinlochbervie' – where else are you going to find that, eh? Should you be needing a hangover cure, the Bloody Marys have been voted one of the five best in Scotland. **Branch: Stravaigin 2** 8 Ruthven Lane, Hellhead, West End (334 7165).

Glasgow: West End

The Ubiquitous Chip ★

12 Ashton Lane (334 5007). Hillhead underground.
Meals served *Restaurant* noon-2.30pm, 5.30-11pm
Mon-Sat; 12.30-3pm, 6.30-11pm Sun. *Brasserie* noon-11pm
Mon-Sat; 12.30-11pm Sun. **Average** *Restaurant* ££££.
Credit AmEx, DC, MC, V.

In 2002, as the Chip was celebrating its 30th birthday, it
collected a Taste of Scotland Award for best city
restaurant in Scotland. Not bad for this grande dame of
Ashton Lane (itself one of the country's classiest eating
and drinking crawls). In fact, the Chip just seems to get
better with age. The main restaurant is housed in a lush
and leafy converted mews, the menu is seductively
Caledonian, the wine list is one of the city's best – and
booking is essential. Sunday lunch is a tradition. The
starters, such as still-sizzling, pan-fried scallops on a
roasted potato cake with stewed garlic and vermouth
sauce, are a hard act to follow. But the main courses –
juicy venison in a gin and juniper berry sauce, for
example – manage to top them. The bar is sometimes
regarded as an outpost of nearby BBC Scotland, busy
with the city's movers, shakers and well-known faces
(and voices); look out for the murals painted by literary
giant Alasdair Gray. Connected to the Chip, but with its
own separate entrance, newish spin-off the Wee Bar is
small, opinionated and very, very Glasgow.

Café-bars & Cafés

The Big Blue

*445 Great Western Road (357 1038). Kelvinbridge
underground.* **Open** noon-11pm Mon-Thur, Sun; noon-
midnight Fri, Sat. **Meals served** noon-3pm, 5-10pm Mon-
Fri; noon-10.30pm Sat, Sun. **Average** ££. **Credit** MC, V.

The best thing about this self-described 'pizza and pasta
bar' is its location: right on Kelvin Bridge, overlooking
the river, which though murky can look positively
Mediterranean on a rare sunny day. As well as the twisty
staircase to the terrace facing the water – look out for the
friendly dolphin statue – there's an entrance on Great
Western Road, which snakes down brightly coloured
tiled walls into a cosy, no-nonsense cellar eating area and
attached bar. The menu is not extensive; pizza, pasta,
shellfish and burgers, which are tasty if not mind-
blowing. The spicy chicken wings make a great snack,
and the profiteroles and other sticky, unhealthy desserts
are hard to resist. It's popular with students (more the
rugby club type than the arts department) and brisk
middle-aged couples, but when the sun's out just about
anyone will head down for an alfresco drink.

Mexican/
American deli
Lupe Pinto's
is at 313
Great Western
Road (334
5444, www.
lupepintos.
com). Owners
Doug Bell
and Rhoda
Robertson,
who opened
the first
branch in
Edinburgh,
recently wrote
a travel/
recipe book
about their
adventures,
*Two Cooks
and a
Suitcase.*

Brel ★

*39-43 Ashton Lane (342 4966/www.brelbarrestaurant.
com). Hillhead underground.* **Open** 10am-midnight daily.
Food served noon-3pm, 5-10pm Mon-Fri; noon-11pm
Sat; noon-10pm Sun. **Average** ££. **Credit** AmEx, DC,
MC, V.

Hewn out of a former stable and named after craggy
Belgian crooner Jacques, Brel is dedicated to the
consumption of other fine Belgian exports: wheat beers
and moules frites. Its distinctive modern-rustic look and
relaxed candlelit ambience has made it an established
fixture of the Ashton Lane drinking scene, attracting a
clientele of trendy but unpretentious bright young things,
including students from neighbouring Glasgow Uni.
There's a laid-back diet of live jazz, rock and pre-club DJs,
as well as a pan-European diet on offer in the neat little
dining area. In the summer, the stable doors are thrown
open and patrons spill out on to the cobbles at the front
or the sloping lawn at the back, clutching their blond
beers and goblets of wine. Well worth a visit for a taste
of West End bohemia.

Firebird ★

1321 Argyle Street (334 0594). Kelvinhall underground.
Open 11.30am-midnight Mon-Thur; 11.30am-1am Fri,
Sat; 11.30am-12.30am Sun. **Average** £. **Credit** MC, V.

This big, airy gastropub is one of the hangouts *du jour*
for Glasgow's twenty- and thirtysomethings. Which is
hardly surprising, since it has managed to pull off, with
some panache, the combination of a chilled, boozy vibe

The Big Blue

and some truly top nosh. Set in the corner of an Argyle Street terrace, Firebird offers views of Kelvingrove Park and Art Gallery from its enormous picture windows. The terracotta stone walls and richly coloured interior make it feel languidly Mediterranean in summer, while in winter the real coal fire and velvety drapes dispel the chill. Pizza is the house speciality, with zippy and fairly unorthodox toppings: wild mushroom and dolcelatte, Mediterranean vegetable, and spinach and potato are some of the options. But if you don't fancy chomping your way through an unstintingly generous helping of crispy pizza, there are alternative main meat courses, and a fish and pasta dish of the day. At weekends, a DJ adds to the general hubbub.

Grassroots Café ★

97 St George's Road (333 0534). St George's Cross underground. **Open** 10am-10pm daily. **Average** £. **Credit** AmEx, MC, V.

For our money, this bijou – and award-winning – café is the best veggie option in the city. It's also one of very few places where your coffee will be made from dandelions. Other than that, it's not especially hippie-dippy, just a laid-back, comfy hangout serving hearty, wholemeal nosh. The vegetarian/vegan menu is handled with skill

Firebird. *See p193.*

Roots & Fruits (475 Great Western Road, 334 3530, and 351 Byres Road, 339 5164) is an excellent fruit and veg merchant with a good organic range. They also sell fruit juices, fresh soups and salads.

and imagination, and offers more than the standard veggie-burger-and-chips scenario (although this option, like the veggie bangers 'n' mash, is spot on, especially after a night on the West End tiles). Equally satisfying lunch or dinner options are the fluffy risotto cakes and the fragrant Thai green curry. For a sugar fix, there's a robust selection of freshly made cakes. Although it overlooks the none-too-attractive M8 at the busy Charing Cross junction, you wouldn't know that inside, where young mothers, aspiring writers and art students converge for a meat-free bonanza – or just some camomile tea and a squint at the day's newspapers.

Insomnia

The Bear Pit, 38 Woodlands Road (564 1800).
St George's Cross underground. **Open** noon-11.15pm Mon-Wed; noon Thur-11.5pm Sun. **Average** £. **Credit** AmEx, MC, V.

Originally opened to much hype as Glasgow's first 24-hour café, and located across the road, some retrenchment and reorganisation has meant that Insomnia is now 'hosted' by the Bear Pit, a cellar bar pitched at students. The trad-looking venue is not entirely authentic (stained-glass-effect windows, fake stone walls, decorative-only fireplace), but at least the grub is good and something of the previous café's laid-back, bohemian air survives in the customers' tendencies to sprawl around for hours with newspapers. It's not quite Central Perk, but it would probably like to be. The food is a mixture of the mildly exotic and the filling, with tasty bruschettas, burritos with vegetable fillings, lots of olive-based dishes, salads and the like. There's a different menu at the weekend, including generous brunches and breakfasts.

The Living Room

5 Byres Road (339 8511). Kelvinhall underground.
Open 11am-11pm Mon-Thur, Sun; 11am-midnight Fri, Sat. **Meals served** noon-9pm Mon-Thur, Sun; noon-7pm Fri, Sat. **Average** £. **Credit** MC, V.

Down at the bottom of Byres Road, the Living Room was one of Glasgow's trendiest joints when it opened, but has now settled into a comfortable slot. It's still pretty hip, but more accessible than a full-on style bar. It occupies two rooms – one is laid out café-style; the other, by the main door, is cosier, with benches, sofas and fire – and is quite striking, with bare walls giving it a cavern-like look despite plenty of window light. The laid-back staff contribute to a pretty relaxed atmosphere, with non-intrusive music; many use it as a pre-club hangout. And the food's not bad, with salads, burgers (veggie and meat) and very good chips, though not every item on the menu is always available.

Naked Soup

106 Byres Road (334 6200). Hillhead underground. **Open** 9am-6pm Mon-Sat; noon-5pm Sun. **No credit cards.**
Nothing to do with Jamie Oliver, but the name says it all: if you want soup, they've got it. And not just boring old tomato or lentil flavours either: this compact little café specialises in unusual ingredients and combinations, with usually around eight to choose from (options change weekly). And if you're not sure, for instance, that pacific salmon and noodles or spicy duck are really going to work as a soup, they're happy to let you try a spoonful first. It's certainly superior stuff: chunky, fresh ingredients, no additives. The place can get crowded at lunchtime – there are only a few stools by the bar-style counter – but you can always get a takeaway. Soups are the staple, but there are also warming casseroles, sandwiches, coffee, fresh smoothies and shakes.

Oblomov

372-374 Great Western Road (339 9177). Kelvinbridge underground. **Meals served** 3-11pm Mon-Thur; 3pm-midnight Fri; 11am-midnight Sat; 11am-11pm Sun.
Average £. **Credit** AmEx, MC, V.
The name, from Goncharov's 19th-century satirical Russian novel, was presumably chosen to complement this classy beerhouse/kitchen's original eastern European theme. That's rather gone by the wayside now, but the menu is still full of unusual dishes that mingle international influences, generally to rich, filling effect.

Naked Soup

There are Thai fish cakes, Japanese-style fried chicken and Moroccan vegetable kofta, as well as cheeseburgers, pasta and so on. Be warned: the portions (especially the breakfasts) tend to be huge. The bar area is candle-lit and elegant, especially when a string quartet is playing, as happens on occasion. For full fin-de-siècle glamour, order absinthe and quote Verlaine.

Otago

61 Otago Street (337 2282). Kelvinbridge underground. **Open** 11am-11pm Mon-Sat; noon-11pm Sun. **Meals served** noon-4pm, 5-9pm daily. **Average ££. Credit** MC, V.

Hidden slightly from view, though only two minutes from Great Western Road, this little bistro is regarded with much affection by the bohemian and student populations of the West End. Its plain tables, chairs and wooden floor give it a clean, airy feel, and there are newspapers to browse. Dishes might seem rather basic, but are beautifully presented and seasoned; a simple bruschetta and salad is done so well, you'll relish it more than more complicated options. Vegetarians will be happy, with plenty of interesting items like asparagus risotto topped with red chard and taleggio – though the kitchen can stretch to main meat courses such as roast supreme of guinea fowl in a mustard and white wine sauce. The food can be rich, but there are plenty of starter options for lighter meals, plus a takeaway service. A wee gem.

Pubs & Bars

Ben Nevis

1147 Argyle Street (576 5204). Exhibition Centre rail. **Open** 11am-11pm Mon-Thur; 11am-midnight Fri, Sat; 12.30-11pm Sun. **No credit cards**.

Two worlds collide harmoniously in the Ben Nevis; that of the hardened whisky drinker and the West End bohemian. This traditional old bloke's boozer was given a stylish refit in 1998, but everything from the open fireplace to the exposed stonework still offers earthy Highland appeal. The aged regulars still prop up the bar, nursing their choice of the 70 whiskies on offer, but these days they rub shoulders with a cross-section of younger drinkers. This winter warmer of a pub is a cosy place to seek refuge, whether on your own or during one of the highly social folk sessions.

The Halt

160 Woodlands Road (564 1527). Kelvinbridge or St George's Cross underground. **Open** 11am-midnight Mon-Sat; 12.30pm-midnight Sun. **Credit** MC, V.

Ben Nevis. See p197.

Once a great West End institution, the Halt has declined markedly since its makeover a few years ago, which stripped away much of its traditional shabby charm. However, it's still a reliable hangout, with bags more individuality than your standard chain pub or mega-bar. Students and office workers predominate, though you'll still find the odd anarcho-punk with a dog on a string left. It's bright and airy, with a reassuringly imposing central bar. There's also a snug at the back and a separate room for occasional bands and open-mic acoustic nights. The main bar is dominated by a large TV screen, and the atmosphere becomes livelier during a big game, but not, thankfully, threatening or particularly sectarian (more than you can say for some Glasgow pubs).

McPhabbs

23 Sandyford Place (221 0770). Charing Cross rail.
Open 11am-11pm Mon-Thur; 11am-midnight Fri, Sat; noon-11pm Sun. **Credit** MC, V.
Many people can't quite be bothered making the trip down Sauchiehall Street to McPhabbs (which is lazy, as it's only five minutes away) – maybe that's why it feels like a bit of a cult hangout. Designed like a traditional Glasgow pub, it also has some wackier touches – witty menus, funny signs, idiosyncratic bar staff – which delight its faithful student clientele. The obligatory wee

men watching football on the TV don't seem to object either. McPhabbs specialises in whacking great plates of grub; most scrummy is the Desperate Dan-like sausages and mash, which comes in a giant soup bowl with lashings of tasty onion gravy. The full breakfasts are certainly full, and you can also get home-made burgers, baked potatoes, chips and the like. There's a patio out back for the occasional sunny day.

Stereo

12-14 Kelvinhaugh Street (576 5018). Exhibition Centre rail. **Open** 5-11pm Mon-Thur; 5pm-midnight Fri; 1pm-midnight Sat; 1-11pm Sun. **Credit** AmEx, MC, V.

Made from girders

To those who haven't grown up in Scotland, Irn-Bru is a disturbingly orange-coloured, tooth-rotting fizzy drink. To most of those who have, it's a way of life, as much a part of the Scottish national identity as sleeping through 1 January or supporting whoever's playing England at football.

As the marketing has it, it's Scotland's *other* national drink and is best known for its allegedly restorative properties the morning after a heavy session. While there doesn't seem to be any scientific basis for its use as a hangover cure, it's certainly true that after a can of Irn-Bru, accompanied perhaps by a roll and square sausage lathered in brown sauce, even Rab C Nesbitt could feel quite human again.

Here are some crucial Irn-Bru statistics:
● It's the biggest selling grocery brand in Scotland.

● Originally mixed in 1901 by Robert Barr, whose family still heads the company.
● First known as Iron Brew, the name was changed to meet food description laws in 1946, thus causing generations of Scots to grow up as bad spellers.
● The exact combination of 32 syrups and flavourings is still a deadly secret, known to only two members of the board.
● The slogan 'Made in Scotland from girders' is, in fact, true: the mixture of ingredients includes 0.002% ammonium ferric citrate.
● Irn-Bru is the only drink in the world that outsells Coca-Cola – in Scotland, that is.
● It's much more common in Moscow than London; Russians, possibly because of their notorious consumption of vodka, have taken it to their hearts. It may yet become their 'other' national drink too.

Glasgow: West End

This alternative, student-friendly bar is the sister venture of Mono (*see p164*) in the Merchant City and, as the name suggests, music is a big part of its attraction. Gigs take place Monday to Wednesday when, for a minimal entry fee, you can enjoy an eclectic mix of local rock, indie, punk and electronica acts and the occasional touring band from overseas. At the weekend, the emphasis shifts to the super-tasty vegan bar menu, comprising filling snacks such as roasted vegetables on bruschetta. Stereo is also a handy stop-off before or after a concert at the SECC (Scottish Exhibition & Conference Centre).

Tap Bar & Coffee Huis

1055 Sauchiehall Street (339 0643). Kelvinbridge underground. **Open** noon-11pm Mon-Thur, Sun; noon-midnight Fri, Sat. **Credit** AmEx, DC, MC, V.

In a great location, overlooking the park and Kelvingrove Art Gallery, the Tap (formerly the Brewery Tap) is an institution beloved of generations of ale drinkers and recently refreshed with a lighter atmosphere and, as the name suggests, good coffee. The two bar areas are bright and airy but still cosy, and punters tend to be a mix of the less rowdy student contingent from the university just across Kelvin Way and more mature West Enders seeking a quiet night out. The Tap is big on music, with regular jazz events, and it's a great place to while away a Sunday afternoon.

Uisge Beatha ★

232 Woodlands Road (564 1596/www.uisgebeathabar. co.uk). Kelvinbridge underground. **Open** noon-midnight Mon-Sat; 12.30pm-midnight Sun. **Credit** (food only) AmEx, MC, V.

The name (pronounced 'ishker-vah') means 'water of life' which, you may know, is Gaelic for whisky – no jokes, please. But this unique bar is not just for folkie types, though they do have an extensive selection of life-water on the premises. You could almost describe this as a Scottish theme pub, but that's not, in this case, a criticism. There may be stuffed animal heads on the walls, countryish pictures and ornaments, squashy chairs and sofas patterned in tartan. And, yes, the bar staff do wear kilts (and very fetching they can look too). But somehow, it isn't too tacky. Maybe that's because the Highland in-fluence is more whimsical than clichéd, or maybe it's just because this is a real pub with genuine local regulars. Still, tourists should get a kick out of it. In keeping with the surroundings, the bar food is full of Scots specialities – this could be the place you finally try haggis. There are hearty breakfasts at weekends and 'comfort food' that's ideal for the fragile and hungover, as well as real ales for those hoping to be.

Glasgow: Southside

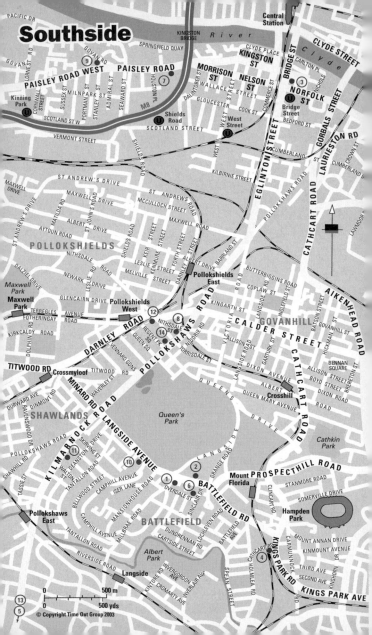

The sprawling Southside is a predominantly residential area dotted with several large parks and museums, including the Burrell Collection of fine art and Charles Rennie Mackintosh's House for an Art Lover. The tenements and high-rise flats of the inner districts gradually give way to suburban communities and housing estates, where restaurants and bars are of mainly local appeal. However, there are also some hallowed old favourites and hip new arrivals. For the greatest concentration of quality dining options, head to the upwardly mobile districts of Pollokshields, Shawlands and Giffnock.

Restaurants

Mediterranean

The Battlefield Rest

55 Battlefield Road (636 6955/www.battlefieldrest.co.uk). Bus 44, 66. **Meals served** noon-3pm, 6-10pm Mon-Sat. **Average** £££. **Credit** AmEx, MC, V.

The beautiful listed building that houses this eagerly patronised Italian restaurant used to be a tram shelter, and its tiled exterior still projects turn-of-the-20th-century class. These days, busy bus routes converge outside but inside all is rosy and cosy – sometimes too cosy, as the tables are closely clustered to meet demand. Italian purists looking for authentic regional cuisine will probably be disappointed. Main courses are strictly pizza, pasta and what is termed 'the Traditional Corner', a little oasis of old British standbys (such as beef medallions) for those who think a ciabatta is something to do with classical music. But within these categories there lie some

Glasgow: Southside

The Battlefield Rest.
See p203.

tempting combinations. The linguine scozzese involves
Arbroath smokies and leeks in a cream sauce, while the
pizza piemontese is topped with sun-dried tomatoes,
onions, spinach and roast peppers.

Café Serghei
67 Bridge Street (429 1547). Bridge Street undergound.
Meals served noon-2.30pm, 5-11pm Mon-Sat; 6-11pm
Sun. **Average** £. **Credit** AmEx, MC, V.
Fancy some theatrical plate-breaking or Zorba-style
dancing with the waiters? Refusing to participate is not
an option at Café Serghei's Friday Greek evenings –
although, in culinary terms, every night is Greek night in
these opulent, cavernous premises. Situated a stone's
throw from the river on the less-than-salubrious Bridge
Street, a different, stately world of pillars, balconies and
domes lies inside this former bank headquarters. The
setting can be quite imposing on a quiet night, but the
hospitality of the staff makes for a warm experience. The
menu encompasses the Greek standards – meze,
dolmádes, kléftiko – at a pre-theatre price of £7 for two
courses. If you want to join the Greek evening, four
courses and entertainment will cost you a bargain £17.50.

The Greek Golden Kebab ★
34 Sinclair Drive (649 7581). Crossmyloof rail.
Meals served 5pm-1am Thur-Sun. **Average** £.
No credit cards.
Although its name is redolent of a greasy takeaway
selling Glasgow's favourite post-pub grub, the Greek
Golden Kebab is actually an unassuming but very
welcoming little family-run restaurant, which has quietly
built up a glowing local reputation over its three decades

**James
McKechnie
& Son** (350
Scotland
Street, 429
1609) is a
gourmet
fishmonger
that supplies
fresh Scottish
produce to
Amaryllis (*see
p184*), **Gamba**
(*see p145*) and
Gleneagles
Hotel chef
Andrew Fairlie.

of service to eastern Mediterranean cuisine. Glasgow is not hugely endowed with Greek restaurants, and this is one of its best. Its busy decor – plastic vine leaves hang on trellises and Med ephemera adorns the walls – is kitsch but charming. The food, covering every Greek dish known to man plus a few less familiar creations, is generally proclaimed to be delicious, with reliable faves such as keftédes and dolmádes available as starters or mains. There is considerable provision for vegetarians. And if you really can't resist a classic chicken or lamb kebab after a night on the tiles, the takeaway service offers many of the dishes on the main menu.

La Fiorentina

2 Paisley Road West (420 1585). Kinning Park underground. **Meals served** noon-2.15pm, 5.30-10.15pm Mon-Sat; noon-2.15pm, 5.30-9.30pm Sun. **Average** ££. **Credit** AmEx, DC, MC, V.

Tucked away in Govan, not far from the all-singing, all-dancing Springfield Quay riverside complex and directly over the road from the uniquely Glaswegian country and western experience of the Grand Ole Opry, this has become a Southside stalwart, thanks to its combination of home-style Tuscan cuisine and the bustling vibe of an authentic Italian trattoria. The jumbled layout, faux rustic touches and odd cheesy mural provide a refreshing antidote to the burgeoning style-over-content ethos. The food reflects the same no-nonsense approach. Simple favourites such as grilled fresh fish in olive oil and herbs, and sautéd or pan-fried escalopes of veal or pork attract a dedicated crowd of salt-of-the-earth Southsiders (Sir Alex Ferguson is from these parts, you know). Also rating a special mention is the risotto: one of the best in the city. A good barolo or amarone wine won't set you back too much either.

Modern European

Ivory

2 Camphill Avenue (636 0223/www.ivoryhotel.com). Bus 45, 48, 57. **Meals served** noon-9.30pm Mon-Thur, Sun; noon-10pm Fri, Sat. **Average** ££. **Credit** MC, V.

Ivory has been an instant hit with the Shawlands/Langside drinking and dining set. Even though you could easily find its match in the city centre, style bars and restaurants are still a relative novelty south of the river, and Ivory's conservatory, overlooking Queen's Park, is never empty. Diners can choose between the view or the intimacy of a booth in the main restaurant, where food options are eclectic and lip-smacking. Starters on the seasonal menu might include stuffed beef tomatoes or mussels, followed by such mains as medallions of duck

Southbank

breast with egg noodles and pak choi, seared salmon on parmesan polenta cakes and a number of steak/pizza/pasta/salad options, all at Southside prices. The two-course set lunch is £7.25; the pre-theatre menu £8.25. Although the adjoining bar is not especially remarkable, it manages to be simultaneously spacious and cosy.

Southbank

2 Mains Avenue (621 2288/www.southbankrestaurant. co.uk). Giffnock rail/bus 38. **Meals served** noon-2pm, 5.30-9.30pm daily. **Average** ££. **Credit** AmEx, MC, V.
The denizens of Giffnock know how to lap up a stylish new enterprise; Southbank had only been open a few months before it was fully booked at weekends. Maybe the patrons were hoping for a glimpse of TV's home makeover queen Carol Smillie – her husband, Alex Knight, is the owner. Southbank doesn't have the distinctive character of the nearby Cook's Room (see below); rather, it is a splash of city-centre finesse, with modish cuisine to match, in the deepest Southside. The interior bears no relation to the premises' former incarnation as a bank, opting instead for a tasteful union of exposed stonework, polished floors, scarlet upholstery and culinary-themed photos through its two rooms. As with many a new contender, the menu plays safe but sure

Website **www. 5pm.co.uk** provides daily info on last-minute dinner deals at restaurants in both Glasgow and Edinburgh. Tables must be booked online by – you guessed it – 5pm.

with its democratic mix of meat, fish and vegetarian dishes, the ubiquitous risotto and a plenitude of drizzled oils and meticulous garnishes.

Scottish

The Cook's Room ★

205 Fenwick Road (621 1903). Giffnock rail. **Meals served** 6pm-midnight Mon-Fri; noon-3pm, 6pm-midnight Sat, Sun. **Average** ££. **Credit** MC, V.
Situated in affluent Giffnock, but worth the taxi ride just outside the Glasgow city boundary, the intimate Cook's Room is a beautifully judged dining experience and the discerning choice for neighbourhood gourmands. The decor is understated – baby-blue walls, a white-tiled range in the corner, padded church pews for seating – so most of the attention goes into the seasonal menu and additional touches such as the complimentary scone appetisers. There are six options per course, including game, fish and vegetarian choices. Starters can range from lip-smacking herb houmous to the staunch Scottish flavours of cullen skink and warm black pudding and pear salad, while mains include duck breast, fillet of halibut and succulent steaks. There are also comforting home-cooked desserts.

Café-bars & Cafés

Agenda

15 Millbrae Road (649 6861). Langside rail. **Open** noon-11pm Mon-Thur, Sun; noon-midnight Fri, Sat. **Average** ££. **Credit** MC, V.

Agenda enjoys a hilltop location overlooking the Langside Monument, Queen's Park and the brooding presence of the Victoria Infirmary. Inside the attractive, industrial grey, brick-and-glass-tiled exterior of this former utility building is a popular bar frequented by locals who enjoy a spot of traditional boozing (and a Thursday night quiz) in chic, uncluttered, modern surroundings. The adjacent restaurant offers a two-course lunch for £7.95 and a pre-theatre deal for £8.95 (even though there are no theatres in the vicinity). The menu offers a catch-all selection of pizzas, pasta, sandwiches, steaks, fowl and fajitas. In some respects, Agenda apes the style bars and restaurants of the more cosmopolitan city centre, but it retains the unpretentious atmosphere of a local hangout. It also operates a daytime play area for kids.

Harry Ramsden's

251 Paisley Road (429 3700/www.harryramsdens.co.uk). Cessnock underground. **Meals served** 7-10am, noon-10pm Mon-Thur; 7-10am, noon-11pm Fri; 8-10am, noon-11pm Sat; 8-10am, noon-10pm Sun. **Average** £. **Credit** AmEx, MC, V.

There's something about Harry's that makes you think you're crossing the ocean on a cruise ship. A pretty luxurious one, mind, with gilt, chandeliers and velvet giving a grand dining room feel and subconsciously making you wonder where the captain's table is. The happily queueing family crowd obviously regard it as a special treat. The service is partly responsible – the staff are excellent – and there's a general attempt to make the dining experience as nice as possible. But it's not a posh night out: the menu is traditional and a tad basic, and prices are very reasonable. Most come for the fish 'n' chips specials, and so they should, as they're delicious: thick-cut, non-greasy chips, good, fresh-tasting fish in crispy batter, proper mushy peas, thinly buttered bread. The ideal fish supper. There are special offers for pensioners and kids, and Harry's is neatly placed for a night at the nearby Odeon multiplex.

Republic Bier Stube

87 Kilmarnock Road (649 5121/www.rbh.info). Pollokshaws East rail/bus 38. **Open** noon-11pm Mon-Thur, Sun; noon-midnight Fri, Sat. **Meals served** noon-10pm daily. **Average** £. **Credit** MC, V.

For a uniquely West of Scotland liquor experience, the reckless drink **Buckfast**. This sickly sweet, highly alcoholic tonic wine, made by the monks of Buckfast Abbey, is the beverage of choice among local, ahem, streetwise youths.

The recent arrival of Republic Bier Stube – German for 'the best thing to happen to hip Southside drinking in an age' – on Shawlands' main drag is a sure indication that the area is starting to shake off its limited nightlife spectrum and cater for the diversity of tastes in the district. Like Republic Bier Halle (see p165), its city-centre sister establishment with which it shares its eastern European theme and stylised beer-hall look, the Stube is more than a bar – the food is worth sampling in its own right. The menu includes filling beef or vegetarian goulash, frankfurter hot dog with sauerkraut, and pizzas and paninis with unusual toppings/fillings such as hoi sin crispy duck or chorizo and gruyère. Wash it all down with a two-pint stein of European lager or a shot from the extensive range of vodkas and schnapps.

The Taverna
778 Pollokshaws Road (424 0858). Queens Park rail.
Open 11am-11pm Mon-Thur; 11am-midnight Fri; noon-midnight Sat; 12.30-11pm Sun. **Meals served** noon-9pm Mon-Sat; 1-9pm Sun. **Credit** MC, V.

The best restaurants

Amaryllis
Gordon Ramsay's Glaswegian odyssey is justly fêted – pricey, but you're worth it. *See p184.*

Café Gandolfi
Canny Caledonian cuisine in distinctive surroundings. *See p154.*

The Cook's Room
Wholesome Scottish home cooking. Complimentary scones too. *See p207.*

Fratelli Sarti
Authentic Italian deli/restaurant bursting with character and customers. *See p146.*

Gamba
Award-winning fish restaurant. *See p145.*

Mother India
Join the regulars for curry heaven. *See p182.*

Stravaigin
Think globally, eat locally at this exceptional bistro. *See p190.*

Glasgow: Southside

At one time, the Taverna was the Athena Greek Taverna, a Greek restaurant-cum-bohemian wine bar; then the proprietors knocked down the partition and merged the two distinct halves into one bright, welcoming café-bar. The turquoise and terracotta colour scheme, ceramic borders, wrought-iron candle holders climbing like ivy around pillars, colourful abstract art on the walls and a bit of foliage in the corner might sound overpowering, but really it's not. It's the kind of place where you can happily while away the hours, day or night – so it's a good job they offer the usual range of bar food (with specials for under a fiver) and a Sunday brunch.

Pubs & Bars

Clockwork Beer Company

1153-1155 Cathcart Road (649 0184). Mount Florida rail. **Open** 11am-11pm Mon-Thur, Sun; 11am-midnight Fri, Sat. **Meals served** 11am-8.45pm Mon-Thur; 11am-9.45pm Fri-Sun. **Credit** DC, MC, V.

The Clockwork is a sizeable neighbourhood watering hole with the homogenous look of a Wetherspoon's or a Hogshead chain pub, which serves the populous Mount Florida/King's Park/Cathcart/Battlefield axis of ale drinkers with beers from its own microbrewery. The wide selection of cask-conditioned draught ales means you need never resort to drinking 'cooking' lager. The adventurous, or just girly, are directed to a glass of the exotic, fruity Hazy Daze ale. Family- and school reunion-friendly, the Clockwork is also used as a pre-match hangout for literally tens of Queen's Park FC supporters fortifying themselves before another valiant display at nearby Hampden Park.

Heraghty's

708 Pollokshaws Road (423 0380). Queens Park rail. **Open** 11am-11pm Mon-Thur; 11am-midnight Fri, Sat; 12.30-11pm Sun. **No credit cards.**

Family-run Heraghty's is a Southside – nay, citywide – institution, as mythologised in the writings of Glasgow Herald scribe Jack 'the urban Voltaire' McLean. If you want to sample grassroots urban pub life as cherished by hard-drinking Glaswegians of a certain vintage, this is as righteous a spit-and-sawdust joint as you could hope for. Behind the etched-glass windows and traditional façade lies a venerable old man's boozer, where regulars decompose in the corners and everybody knows your name, unless you're not from round these parts. So do think twice before trying to order an alcopop. Food is not available.

Samuel Dow's

69-71 Nithsdale Road (423 0107). Pollokshaws West rail.
Open 11am-11pm Mon-Thur, Sun; 11am-midnight Fri,
Sat. **No credit cards**.

Another comfy, locally renowned hostelry with its fair
share of characters propping up the bar. Sammy Dow's
adheres to trad pub values, although it has succumbed
to the nefarious consumer attractions of drinks promos
and a quiz night (Tuesday, since you ask). There's also a
weekly jam session (Thursday), rock and pop cover bands
(Friday and Saturday), jazz (Sunday afternoon) and a
poetry meeting (first Monday of the month).

Heraghty's

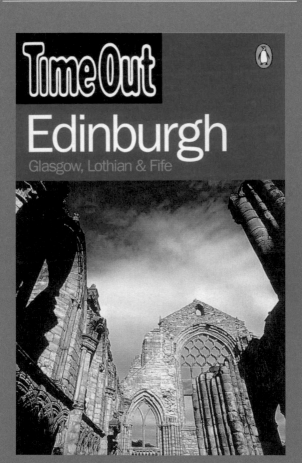

Where to…

Index

Index

Index

Index

Ad Index

Please refer to the relevant pages
for addresses and telephone numbers.